How to Be in a Personal Relationship

Skills for Beginning, Strengthening, and Maintaining an Intimate Personal Relationship

Stephen J. Sampson, Ph.D.
Cindy Elrod, Ph.D.

HRD Press, Inc. • Amherst • Massachusetts

Published by: HRD Press, Inc.
                  22 Amherst Road
                  Amherst, MA 01002
                  800-822-2801 (U.S. and Canada)
                  413-253-3488
                  413-253-3490 (fax)
                  www.hrdpress.com

ISBN 978-1-59996-065-4

Production services by Jean Miller
Cover design by Eileen Klockars
Editorial work by Sally M. Farnham

Table of Contents

Acknowledgments

It is with gratitude and appreciation that the authors would like to acknowledge the contributions of the following individuals for their time, energy, feedback, and support during the process of writing this book:

Robert Carkhuff, Sr., Ph.D., for laying the foundation for the work presented here and for his personal support of this project.

Jack Blakeman, Ph.D., for his long-time mentoring and modeling of these skills.

Jan Sampson, Steve's life partner, whose patience and commitment to the values of partnership and family taught Steve what is really important.

Kerrie Warren Sampson for her help and support in preparing the manuscript.

All the researchers and scientists who have worked (and are *still* working tirelessly) toward the knowledge base of Human Technology, social and emotional intelligence, and all the topics and disciplines that help us understand the many complexities of human interactions.

And finally, to the many family members, friends, colleagues, and workshop participants who read, reread, and read again various versions and layouts of the material and then provided us with invaluable and honest feedback.

The greatest gifts are the gifts of time and teaching. We thank you *all* for your time, and we are humbled by what you have taught us about being in a personal relationship.

About the Authors

Stephen J. Sampson has a Ph.D. in Counseling Psychology from Georgia State University (GSU) and is a Master Trainer in Interpersonal Communications Skills. As an educator, he is a former assistant professor of criminal justice and a retired clinical professor of counseling and psychological services at GSU. He has been teaching conflict resolution and interpersonal skills for over 30 years and has conducted training in interpersonal skills to over 200 agencies and organizations in 35 states.

As a psychologist, Steve is the former chief of psychology at Georgia Regional Hospital and is a contract psychologist with the Georgia State Patrol and 15 metropolitan Atlanta law enforcement agencies. Besides training and testing, he conducts "fitness for duty" evaluations and post shooting debriefings. He is a nationally recognized mediator in workplace violence.

Steve's background as a criminologist includes being the former correctional superintendent of Massachusetts Halfway Houses, Inc. and the former correctional superintendent for the Georgia Department of Corrections. He is a member of the Editorial Review Board for *Correctional Management Reporter*. Steve has provided training consultation to over 150 law enforcement and correctional agencies throughout the United States.

Cindy Elrod holds a Ph.D. in Community/Organizational Psychology from Georgia State University (GSU) where, as a visiting lecturer and instructor, she taught a variety of classes including group process and dynamics, behavior modification, learning, abnormal psychology, and environmental and social influences on behavior.

An established researcher, she has investigated human responses to transitions, psychological contracts, job satisfaction, followership, organizational character, as well as social participation, social support, and sense of community among elders. At the National Center for Post-Traumatic Stress Disorder, she investigated the Federal Emergency Management Agency's (FEMA) process for implementing a disaster mental health response program in communities with disaster declarations (see *The Annals of the American Academy of Political and Social Science*, March 2006).

Cindy came to the consulting, academic, and research environments after 22 years in the airline industry in field operations where she resolved over 15,500 customer complaints; authored and implemented training in conflict negotiation, emergency preparedness and response, and frontline leadership basics; and led operational teams into active airline disaster areas. She has consulted and worked in a variety of settings conducting job analyses, customer service training, and program evaluations.

Steve Sampson is the founder and president of **SoTelligence,**™ **Inc.,** a company created to bring the practical technology of skills-based training into the world of human interactions and relations.

SoTelligence™ teaches you the skills necessary to become a social technologist, able to develop, grow, and maintain healthy relationships in the workplace, in the home, and in any social situation.

SoTelligence™ brings you a series of skills-oriented courses, books, and DVDs—no "shoulds" or "oughts"—just practical, applicable skills that are *immediately useful*. The program is realistic. It is not designed to take the place of the fundamental *technical* skills you need to do your job or interact with family and friends. It is designed to complement those technical skills by *adding* social intelligence training to your skills set so that where and when you choose to use it, it will be there.

For more information, please visit us at **www.SoTelligence.com.**

How to Be in a Personal Relationship

Preface

If you are reading this section, it means that you have taken the time to at least pick up this book, and you have at least a little curiosity about what it might be about. You may be standing in the aisle of the bookstore asking yourself the question, "There are so many books out there on relationships. What's going to make this one different?" That's a great question, and one that deserves an answer. So, read on and we'll tell you a little about the thinking behind this book.

Most of the books that we've come across have been written from the standpoint of the author giving you lots of information. These books have been full of text explaining theories, ideas, concepts, and thoughts about how to find and/or maintain "love." And a very few books have included other resources like websites to visit or short surveys or checklists intended to give you "insight," or self knowledge, about how you interact with others or what you want in a relationship or what you **don't** want in a relationship. But we've not been able to find any book on relationships that combines the presentation of knowledge with actual skill-building activities specifically written to guide you toward making changes in your behaviors that will help you begin, strengthen, and maintain your relationships with a romantic partner. Knowledge is great, but knowledge doesn't become **powerful** until it begins to motivate you to make changes in your behaviors. The purpose of this book is to fill the gap between giving you knowledge and making that knowledge powerful for you.

The teachings of this book are based on something called **Human Technology**, a concept coined and developed in the 1960s by the preeminent researcher, psychologist, and scholar Robert Carkhuff, Sr., Ph.D. Dr. Carkhuff developed a model for the study of (**-ology**) the **techn**iques for being **human**. Scholars and practitioners have since spoken of this model as skills-based training for how to be *humane*.

Think of it this way. Most teaching is done from a "theorist" perspective. Someone stands before you (think of your classroom settings) and teaches you about the "what" of things. Theorists use concepts to explain theories. They talk to you about the "ideal" situation, or what the situation "should" be. Their goal is to give you knowledge by influencing your thoughts. Then, they measure how well you've learned the material by asking you to "tell me" using your words, either written or spoken. A Technologist works a little differently. A Technologist teaches you about the "how" of things. They avoid "fuzzy terms" and use concrete and specific definitions to explain concepts so that a person can actually apply the concept to their life. They talk in terms of the "realized," or real world situations. Their goal is to provide you with skills that will influence and shape your behaviors. They measure how well you've learned by asking you to "show me" using your actions to demonstrate your knowledge. The following diagram might help demonstrate this.

Theorist		Technologist
"What"	*teaches the*	"How"
concepts	*They use...*	concrete and specific definitions
theories	*to explain...*	applications
idealized	*They talk in terms of the...*	realized
knowledge	*Their goal is to give you...*	skills
thoughts	*by influencing your...*	behaviors
tell me	*They measure how well you've learned by asking you to...*	show me
words	*using your...*	actions

This book is written from the "technologist" perspective. It is skills-based training that breaks each of the concepts down into very basic skills that you will have the chance to learn individually. These small skills act as building blocks. In other words, once you learn a skill, you move on to the next skill that will *build* on the skills you have learned up to that point. You will be guided through this step-wise progression using diagrams of how each of the skills fits together and what smaller sub-skills make up each skill. For example, here is a diagram of the three sub-skills of the skill "Looking Carefully" in the Visual Awareness

How to Be in a Personal Relationship

section of the Mental Attending skills chapter located in Section I of the book, How to Pay Skilled Attention.

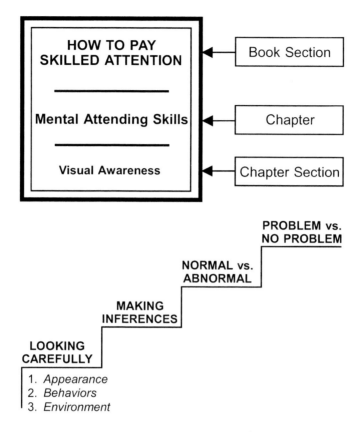

Each skill is introduced, explained, and defined at the beginning of its section. We then "demonstrate" these concepts using short stories called Making the Point. These stories are based on real world examples, some of which may be very familiar to you. Additionally, we provide you with concrete and specific definitions for each skill. These can be found inside a bordered box in each section. Here's an example:

> **CONCRETE AND SPECIFIC DEFINITIONS** for each skill can be found in these boxes.

We also include practice sessions where you are asked to reflect on the material that has just been presented and then think about how that material relates to your life, and you are encouraged to use real life scenarios that have happened to you. For example, in the section on Gesturing, you are asked to list three unattractive gestures that you make when talking with others that you would like to change. If you can't think of one, we provide examples to help you open your mind.

At the end of each section, we have provided you with a section called Action Strategies. In this section, we will present you with several short scenarios that reflect the skills you have just learned about in that section. Following each scenario, we provide you with concrete and specific behaviors that you can apply as a part of your response to the situation. We also give you a chance to come up with your own scenario and action strategy to provide you with even more practice for each of the skills.

Finally, throughout the book, you will find blocks that indicate a DVD followed by the title of the section of the video that is appropriate for that particular section of the book (e.g., DVD: Arranging—The Wrong Way and the Right Way). A DVD has been provided with this book that will further provide you with demonstrations of each of the skills in real world situations. This takes the concepts out of the book and provides you with human behaviors that you can study and adapt to your own skills. It also gives you the opportunity to observe some of the subtle behaviors that can influence the communication you have with your partner that simply cannot be described sufficiently using words.

Now that you have a general understanding of how this book is put together, we invite you to turn the page and start developing the skills that will lead you to more satisfying interactions with your personal relationships.

Introduction

Learning Fundamental Skills for Loving

We know that attraction to others is not something you can force, and we assume that nature probably plays a big part in this. Yet, even when we are strongly attracted to someone, we know that attraction tends to decrease over time as the "newness" wears off (i.e., we become "used" to each other). We have also come to believe that our attraction decreases over time due to our lack of the knowledge and skills necessary to *maintain* passion and love for someone else. To maintain a commitment to *anything* requires having the skills and knowledge to keep nature from ruling and to keep "newness" alive.

One of the authors remembers the time when an elderly gentleman in a very old automobile that looked brand new pulled up beside him. The author asked the gentleman how old the car was. "Thirty-five years," came the reply. Another question followed, "When did you buy it?" The man replied using a tone of voice that seemed to indicate he was annoyed with the question, "I bought it new." The questions continued, "How many miles are on the car?" The gentleman reflected, "I lost count several years ago, but probably around 300,000 miles." This certainly begged a final question, "How did you keep it looking so new?" to which the man simply replied, "I love it, and I attend to it."

This man had said something profound. First, he declared his passion for his car, "I love it." Second, he acknowledged that he knew he had to perform the necessary tasks to keep it looking and operating like new. "I love it, and I attend to it."

This book attempts to help you do the same thing. The goal is to help you discover and maintain the passion and love that you feel for someone by using knowledge and skills to keep it alive and new. "I love (him/her), and I attend to (him/her)."

Many of the skills in this book are applicable to all types of relationships: parenting, family, friendships, and anywhere social and emotional closeness are the goal. However, this book will focus on personal relationships where the goal is intimacy. In other words, this book is about relationships where people sleep together, have sexual contact, may have children together, and are "exclusive," meaning there is a personal commitment to that relationship. This exclusiveness generally refers to relationships that involve married couples, engaged couples, or relationships where the partners are committed to each other and do not have other "outside" partners.

Now, we know that personal relationships can be complicated and diverse due to the nature of the partners' unique personalities, needs, life circumstances, ages, and a variety of other factors. But to write one book that addresses *all* of those factors individually would be voluminous and overwhelming. For example, a couple married for 25 years with three children, one of whom has serious mental and physical disabilities, faces different challenges than a couple just married with no children. Unfortunately, it would simply be impossible to address every possible scenario facing an intimate couple.

What this book *will* emphasize are the *fundamental skills* necessary to maintain a positive relationship. The fundamental skills are ones that, if practiced, despite the relationship's uniqueness, can help the partners stay on a positive track. For example, a couple that has financial problems, health problems with one of the partners, and a difficult child to raise must have the fundamental mental, social, and emotional skills necessary to keep their relationship on track in a positive way.

We've subtitled this introduction Learning Fundamental Skills for Loving in order to emphasize the two critical principles of this book. The first principle is that successful long-term relationships require that the persons involved learn how to love. The second principle is that knowing about love is not enough; you must be able to apply that knowledge through skills.

Love is a skill not to be confused with lust. It's not that lust (physical and emotional attraction) isn't a critical component to "jump start" a relationship. But lust, unfortunately, is not enough. Lust ensures that we become involved with the opposite sex to create children. It neither ensures long-term commitment nor protection of our offspring.

Love requires more than lust for relationship success. It requires that people learn to love beyond that first physical attraction. It requires us to learn to love socially, intellectually, and emotionally.

Social love is the way partners talk to each other using their words and body language. This is sometimes called nonverbal communication. For example, *saying* the right thing at the right time to a distressed loved one is a social skill using words, or verbal skills. Giving a hug or a smile to a loved one when you first see him or her is an example of a nonverbal skill.

Intellectual love is the way a partner respects the other partner's knowledge and thinking. For example, one partner may have the kind of knowledge and thinking that makes them really saavy at managing money, whereas the other partner has the kind of knowledge and thinking that makes him or her better at repairing mechanical things when they break. And *together* they bring different knowledge and thoughts to a problem that can help them be more creative and effective solving that problem than if they each tried to tackle the problem alone. In other words, it is the realization that two brains, and their separate stored knowledge, bring more information "to the table" to help solve life's unexpected and complex problems.

Emotional love refers to the way partners respond to each other's emotional needs. It involves the ability to express emotions and receive emotions in a constructive manner. For example, a partner who emotionally loves his or her partner and who has had a difficult day at work and is now coming home tired and distressed does not take it out on the partner. And the other partner respects the emotional state of the tired and distressed partner.

This book will, therefore focus on the social, intellectual, and emotional skills necessary to maintain love in a long-term relationship.

A second critical principle emphasized in this book is skill. We've already mentioned the word *skill* several times. There is a distinct difference between knowledge and skill. Knowledge refers to having information about a subject. For example, you may know a lot about the game of golf or tennis by reading about it and watching it on television. Yet that immense knowledge of the game does not mean you could pick up a golf club or tennis racket and be able to play proficiently.

Skill is the *application* of that knowledge in everyday life. Skill is the *action* that *supports* the knowledge. All too often people read books on marriage and parenting that provide them with information in the form of facts and ideas about marriage and parenting. This new-found knowledge can be helpful, but it is usually short lived. The reason is that new knowledge tends to be lost if it is not acted upon quickly, repeatedly, and accurately. This is caused by several factors.

If knowledge is not acted upon quickly, it does not get converted into a memory, and the information can be lost. If knowledge is not rehearsed repeatedly, the brain tends to lose it due to memory decay. If knowledge is not applied correctly through skills that accurately reflect that knowledge, it is lost due to its failure to accomplish the goal.

For example, you may read in a parenting book that a child should receive immediate negative consequences for inappropriate behavior so that the child will connect the behavior to the consequences. This is sound scientifically, but unfortunately, it has left out several other factors to consider such as your child's reinforcement history, the social style used by the parent while delivering the consequence, the situational factors present when delivering the consequences, the child's personality, and other factors too numerous to mention.

So, it is easy to see how skills are crucial vehicles for applying knowledge. And the success of each skill requires that you know who, what, when, where, why, and how to use it before applying it. Skills are actions. They require more than "book smarts." They require "action smarts." This book presents several skills with examples of good and poor applications. It also stresses that your repertoire of skills increases the probability of successful application. In other words, the more skills you have available to you, the greater your chances of having one available to fit any given situation.

This book utilizes written exercises and case studies to help reinforce your learning and facilitate your thinking beyond just reading. This book also provides an accompanying DVD. You will see several instances that state "DVD" following your reading. These DVDs present the skills discussed so that you can actually see them applied. When you can see something, it greatly increases the possibility of applying it. The DVD also shows good and bad examples of the skills being applied using life-like personal relationship situations that often cause problems if they are not managed using the skills discussed in this book.

A final note of critical importance: the information and skills discussed in this book are based on scientific principles and research. They are not based solely on the actions, unique bias, or prejudices of the authors about how to be in a personal relationship. It has been our experience that all too often, people write books about how to do something based on their own beliefs or limited to their personal life experiences. Although these types of books might contain some valid information, they run the risk of what scientists call over-generalizing. In other words, the writer believes that what works for him or her generalizes to your situations as well as to everyone else's situations. The information and skills in this book are based on a review of scientific literature regarding personal relationship issues.

It is also important to note that the potential for over-generalization can occur from reading *this* book. This is because the amount of knowledge and accompanying complexity regarding personal relationships could never be covered in a single book. We believe that the knowledge and skills discussed in this book can increase the probability of success in your personal relationships. It will be up to *you* when, where, what, how, why, and with whom you choose to use these skills.

For your reference, we have taken all of the skills that will be discussed in this book and put them into a model. This provides a way of organizing the information into a more meaningful "picture" that may help you comprehend and adapt these skills as behaviors in your personal life.

The Model for How to Be
in a Personal Relationship

**THE MODEL FOR HOW TO BE
IN A PERSONAL RELATIONSHIP**

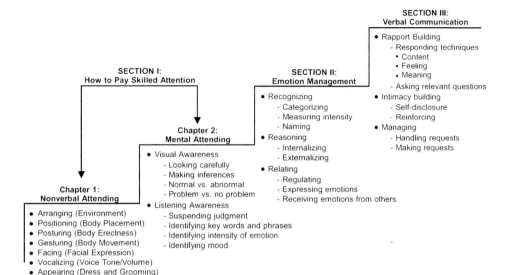

SECTION III:
Verbal Communication

- Rapport Building
  - Responding techniques
    • Content
    • Feeling
    • Meaning
  - Asking relevant questions
- Intimacy building
  - Self-disclosure
  - Reinforcing
- Managing
  - Handling requests
  - Making requests

SECTION I:
How to Pay Skilled Attention

SECTION II:
Emotion Management

- Recognizing
  - Categorizing
  - Measuring intensity
  - Naming
- Reasoning
  - Internalizing
  - Externalizing
- Relating
  - Regulating
  - Expressing emotions
  - Receiving emotions from others

Chapter 2:
Mental Attending

- Visual Awareness
  - Looking carefully
  - Making inferences
  - Normal vs. abnormal
  - Problem vs. no problem
- Listening Awareness
  - Suspending judgment
  - Identifying key words and phrases
  - Identifying intensity of emotion
  - Identifying mood

Chapter 1:
Nonverbal Attending

- Arranging (Environment)
- Positioning (Body Placement)
- Posturing (Body Erectness)
- Gesturing (Body Movement)
- Facing (Facial Expression)
- Vocalizing (Voice Tone/Volume)
- Appearing (Dress and Grooming)
- Touching

Section I

How to Pay Skilled Attention

Paying quality attention to anything is not easy. It requires skills that need to be practiced so the skills become ingrained in you to the point that you do them without thinking. When you pay skilled attention to someone, you are telling them you care about them. Some might even say that the amount of attention you give someone equates to how much you love them.

For example, you care about your friend, Jim or Sue, and you are spending 10 hours a week doing things with and for them. You tell everyone how much you love your spouse or child, but you spend only five hours per week doing things with and for them. Just think, if you are giving your golf or tennis game more attention per week than your loved one, it may speak volumes about what you really care about.

Making the Point—The WRONG Way
The Case of the Rising Star

Jim is a rising star in the Metro Police Department. He has achieved the rank of captain in just 12 years with the department. Jim tells everyone how passionate he is about his chosen profession. He goes in early and stays late at work without being asked. There are rumors floating that he is a likely candidate for the police chief's position when the current chief retires in three years.

It's 8:30 p.m., and Jim is just getting home from work. He is looking forward to the normal dinner his wife, Sue, prepares for him, no matter how late he arrives. Tonight, however, as he enters his home, he senses something is wrong. He calls out his wife's name, but there is no response. He walks into the kitchen and turns on the lights. The lights are always on when he enters his home. He notices a letter on the kitchen table addressed to him.

The letter is from his wife. It is four pages long. It starts out telling Jim she's moved back to her parents' home, and she wants a divorce. The reasons are his lack of attention and his preoccupation with his work. She also mentions Jim's unwillingness to have children until his career is set. She writes to him how lonely she has been the past three years. She adds that she doesn't want any phone calls or contact from him for a while.

Jim is stunned because he didn't see this coming. Jim attempts to call his wife at her parents' after reading the letter. Her father answers and says to Jim that he's sorry, but Sue doesn't want to come to the phone.

Of course, there are a lot of demands on our attention, especially in a complicated society like ours. It is often difficult to know which demand we should give our attention to. They all may seem equally important at times, and we can easily get pulled or distracted. We often worry about money, how our homes look, what automobiles we drive, our health, our appearance, our careers, what people think about us, our pets, our reputation, etc. Any of us could make a list. The problem with all of these competing issues is that they force us to have "divided attention" to a lot of things and no "undivided attention" to the things that truly matter. Many of us want it all, and we tend to think it is all achievable. Unfortunately, that's not likely.

Making the Point—The WRONG Way
The Case of the Perfect Partner

Bonnie wanted it all. She wanted to be a perfect wife, a perfect mother, and a successful executive with a six-figure salary with a perfect figure, a beautiful home, and a great social life. Bonnie was (at least in her mind) managing them all well for the past 20 years. Everything seemed idyllic. It all came to a sad realization on a Friday afternoon when she got a call from a close friend. Bonnie's husband, Sam, had been seen on several occasions with another woman, a neighbor and close friend of Bonnie's. Bonnie didn't want to believe it.

When Sam came home from work that evening, Bonnie confronted him. He initially denied it, but then he admitted it was true. He stated that he had been seeing the neighbor socially for about two months, but nothing sexual had taken place. The neighbor was a widow who had lost her husband two years ago. Sam added that the neighbor was attentive to him and acted like he mattered.

Then Sam brought up the fact that he and Bonnie hadn't slept together in three months. He reminded Bonnie that he had been telling her that they needed to start doing things together without other people being present. Sam then angrily stated that Bonnie was married to her job, and that's all she ever talked about.

Later that evening, Bonnie's daughter, Eliza, called from college. She is Bonnie's daughter from her first marriage. Bonnie's marriage to Sam is marriage number three. Eliza rarely comes home from college other than at Christmas. When Bonnie told Eliza about Sam's relationship with the neighbor, Eliza didn't say anything. Bonnie asked Eliza why she was quiet. Eliza responded that she didn't feel Sam was a bad person. She added that her mother went through the same thing twice before. Both of her previous husbands, including Eliza's dad, had had affairs. Eliza then suggested to Bonnie that she probably shouldn't be married because she is so wrapped up in her career.

(continued)

> Then Eliza said something that shocked Bonnie. Eliza told her mother that one of the reasons she never comes home from college is her mother's preoccupation with her work. The final blow was when Eliza said that Sam paid more attention to her when she was home from college than her mother.

There are two lessons to be learned from Jim's and Bonnie's dilemmas. The first lesson is that you must begin to prioritize those things that matter to you the most, and give those things more attention. Keep in mind that this book's emphasis is on personal relationships, so if your personal relationship is really important to you, then you need to make it a priority and direct a lot of attention to it if you want it to succeed.

The second lesson to be learned is this: most of us will always have multiple things that need our immediate attention, so it benefits us to *learn* how to become better and more efficient at paying attention. Telling someone to observe and listen more carefully to things that matter doesn't mean they can. Telling someone to act like they are paying attention doesn't mean they are. *Teaching* someone to observe, listen, and attend can make a difference. Paying attention is a complicated skill that takes a lot of practice to acquire. Once you have acquired it, you can become more efficient at paying attention to multiple things pulling at you.

The ultimate goal of paying skilled attention is learning to "sense" things accurately and quickly. For example, the quicker you read a person's facial expression or hear the tone of voice behind their words, the better you can gauge your responses to their needs.

It is important to note at this point that, despite how well you pay attention, you can't have it all. In other words, our ability to pay *skilled* attention does not mean you will be able to pay attention to all the things in your life you want to. You have to decide eventually what matters the most, and then let those things go that have some importance to you but ultimately get in the way of those things that matter most.

There are two main components involved in paying skilled attention to others. The first is Nonverbal Attending, and it is composed of eight basic skills: Arranging, Positioning, Posturing, Gesturing, Facing, Vocalizing, Appearing, and Touching. These are discussed in detail in Chapter 1 of this section. The second component of paying skilled attention to others is Mental Attending. Mental Attending involves Visual and Listening Awareness. These skills are discussed in Chapter 2 of this section.

HOW TO PAY SKILLED ATTENTION

Chapter 2:
Mental Attending

- Visual awareness
- Listening awareness

Chapter 1:
Nonverbal Attending

- Arranging (Environment)
- Positioning (Body Placement)
- Posturing (Body Erectness)
- Gesturing (Body Movement)
- Facing (Facial Expression)
- Vocalizing (Voice Tone/Volume)
- Appearing (Dress and Grooming)
- Touching

Let's get started with the Nonverbal Attending skills.

Chapter 1

Nonverbal Attending

Nonverbal attending is the ability to convey without words your attraction to another person. It can be conveyed by simply giving eye contact to someone while they are speaking, or by squaring your body in their direction while they are talking, or by touching them on the shoulder or hand. Nonverbal attending is basically showing someone you care by giving them your undivided attention through the use of body language. We can do this through facial expressions, body placement, tone of voice, touch, and body gestures.

Unfortunately the majority of relationships lose their nonverbal attending patterns for a variety of reasons. It could be that we take the relationship for granted, have had a lot of conflicts that caused nonverbal avoidance of each other, are not attracted to each other, or have simply gotten into the habit of not doing it. When this pattern of *not attending to a loved one* nonverbally starts to occur, it is a major indication that the relationship may be in trouble.

Making the Point—The WRONG Way
The Case of Living Separate Lives

John and Mary have been married for ten years. They have two children, ages four and seven. They both work.

Recently, Mary has started sensing something wrong in their relationship. She and John rarely speak to each other when they are alone, unless it's about family matters. Their typical routine, once the children are in bed: John watches television, and Mary reads in the bedroom.

Mary decides to initiate a conversation with John about her concerns regarding their relationship. She enters the den where John is watching television. As she begins the discussion, John keeps looking at the television, even though he says, "I'm listening." As Mary continues to talk, John starts using the remote to change channels on the television, never breaking eye contact from the television, never making eye contact with Mary, and never turning his body toward Mary while she's talking.

Out of frustration, Mary stands up and says, "I've had it. You're not listening," and she leaves the room in anger. John continues to sit, watching the television as if nothing has occurred.

(continued)

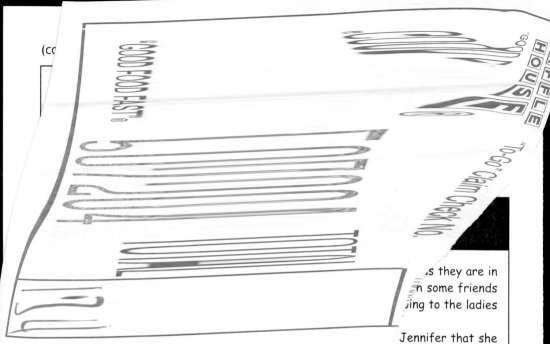

(co

...s they are in
...n some friends
...ing to the ladies

...Jennifer that she
...seems real happy. Jennifer responds that she is. Brittany then says to Jennifer, "Bill can't keep his eyes off you. He looks at you while you're speaking to him, and he has this look on his face of wonderment." Brittany then comments, "I noticed this evening that Bill pulled your chair out for you at dinner and touched you on the shoulder after you sat down." Jennifer smiled and didn't say anything.

As the evening went on, Brittany was observing Jennifer's reactions to Bill. She noticed that Jennifer would become quiet when Bill spoke and looked directly at him. She also noticed Jennifer putting her hand on Bill's hand under the table on several occasions during dinner.

A friend once commented that he liked his dog, a golden retriever, better than any person he knew. He probably had good reason to feel that way because most dogs are always giving and seeking nonverbal attention by wagging their tails, running toward you, and looking at you. When you get angry with a dog it may walk away but will quickly seek your attention again upon seeing you.

Humans, on the other hand, become angry and start to withhold their attention from one another if the other person rejected or ignored them. The person being ignored or rejected will usually start to nonverbally disrespect that person upon seeing them, and the cycle begins. It is difficult to give attention to another person who doesn't reciprocate that attention. Giving and receiving attention at the nonverbal level is the glue, or foundation, for a personal relationship success or failure.

How to Be in a Personal Relationship

There are eight Nonverbal Attending Skills involved in paying skilled attention to others: Arranging, Positioning, Posturing, Gesturing, Facing, Vocalizing, Appearing, and Touching.

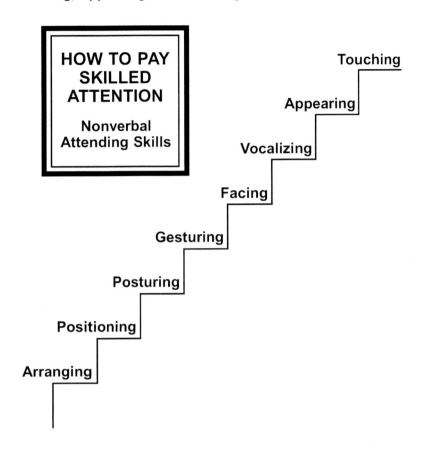

Arranging

How you arrange, or order, the environment in which you talk to your partner contributes to your goal achievement. If you are highly skilled socially, you already know that the arrangement of the environment is an important contributor to the success of your interactions with others. In fact, it probably comes so "naturally" to you that it is often over-shadowed by other skills. For most of us, however, this is an area in which we should expend real effort.

When we examine the behaviors of highly functional people, a dominant trait they share is that they place a lot of significance and importance on details. Arranging sub-skills focus on the details of the environment.

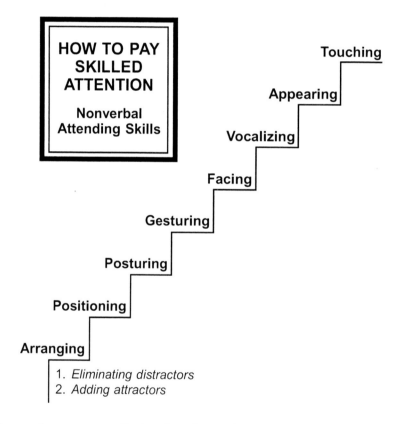

Arranging means eliminating from the environment anything that might distract you or your partner with whom you are talking. A second goal of arranging is to make the environment pleasant and less stressful by adding attractors.

Arranging: Eliminating Distractors

The first principle of arranging is eliminating distractors. Most people have been in an environment where there were many distractors. Remember what it was like to try to talk with your partner when you were in a distracting environment? For both you and your partner, outside noises, uncomfortable chairs, and an uncomfortable room temperature can divert your attention and deplete your energy so that more time is required.

Imagine your home environment where you are trying to talk with your partner. Are there noises that can be eliminated? Can phone calls be eliminated? Is furniture reasonably comfortable? Does the placement of furniture create a barrier? Or is it best to simply remove yourself and your partner with whom you are talking from the distracting environment and talk with them in a quiet environment? Eliminating those distractions is important to successful interactions.

> **ARRANGING** means eliminating from the environment anything that might distract you or your partner while you are interacting with each other.

DVD

ARRANGING: Eliminating Distractors
— The *Wrong* Way and the *Right* Way

Practice

List some distractions you experienced when you were in the presence of your partner and communication was important.

Example: The television was on.

_____

_____

_____

_____

_____

_____

_____

_____

Arranging: Adding Attractors

The second sub-skill of arranging is adding attractors. Following the elimination of distractions, you might consider actually adding *attractors* to the environment. You can enhance your personal environment in order to communicate more effectively. Providing privacy and comfortable furniture and having food may improve your interactions. Your best standard is probably the one you would establish for yourself.

> **ARRANGING** means adding attractors, or enhancements, to the environment that might lead to reduced stress and more effective communication

DVD

ARRANGING: Adding Attractors
— The *Wrong* Way and the *Right* Way

Practice

List some characteristics of a present environment that either contributed to reducing your stress or facilitated your ability to communicate with others.

Example: Back porch with plants and trees.

_____

_____

_____

_____

_____

_____

_____

_____

_____

_____

Making the Point—The WRONG Way
The Case of the TV Lover

Trey and Jackie have been together for six years. Jackie has become aware of Trey's withdrawal from the relationship. When he arrives home, he immediately goes to his shop downstairs. Although he acknowledges Jackie by saying hello, he rarely says anything else.

When Jackie calls him to dinner, he comes up, but rarely says anything. When dinner ends, Trey immediately goes to the den and turns on the television. Jackie comes into the den often and attempts to converse with him. Trey continues to watch TV while Jackie tries to initiate conversation.

Although Trey nods his head while Jackie speaks, he never looks at her and continues to watch TV. Jackie eventually leaves the den, prepares for bed, and reads until falling asleep. Trey usually comes to bed about an hour after Jackie has fallen asleep.

Trey really loves TV.

Making the Point—The RIGHT Way
The Case of the iPod Lover

Jack and Pam have been married for 15 years. They would describe their relationship as very positive. They have two children, ages six and eight.

Every other weekend, their two children spend the weekend with Pam's parents so that Jack and Pam have some time alone. Pam recently bought Jack an iPod with 250 of Jack's favorite songs on it. Jack loves his iPod and always uses it when he takes his daily jog around the neighborhood. Recently, Jack has gotten into the habit of wearing his iPod around the house.

It is now the weekend that their children are with Pam's parents. Jack has come in from jogging and keeps his iPod on as he walks around the house. Pam attempts to talk with Jack about how she would like the weekend to be. Jack does not acknowledge her and continues to listen to his iPod. Pam makes another attempt to talk with Jack, but he still doesn't acknowledge her. He continues to listen to his iPod.

Pam walks out of the room to the kitchen. Jack observes this. He follows Pam into the kitchen and immediately takes off his headphones. He places the iPod on the kitchen counter and tells Pam he's sorry. Jack then asks Pam to sit down at the kitchen table and begins to talk to her about how she would like the weekend to go.

Jack really loves Pam.

Action Strategies

Below are some Arranging Strategies you may want to use in your personal relationships if the situation allows for it.

1. Your partner approaches you while you are watching TV.
    Turn off the TV and put down the remote control.

2. You are working on your computer and your partner enters the room and says hello.
    Turn off the computer and pull up a chair for them to sit in.

3. You have just finished dinner with your partner.
    Help them clean up and suggest that you both take a walk afterward.

4. You are entering a restaurant with your partner.
    Request a table in the restaurant that gives you a lot of privacy.

5. You are sitting on the porch when your partner comes up and wants to talk.
    Get up and get a chair. Place the chair across from you and ask your partner to sit.

Now, write an Arranging Action Strategy:

_____

_____

_____

_____

_____

_____

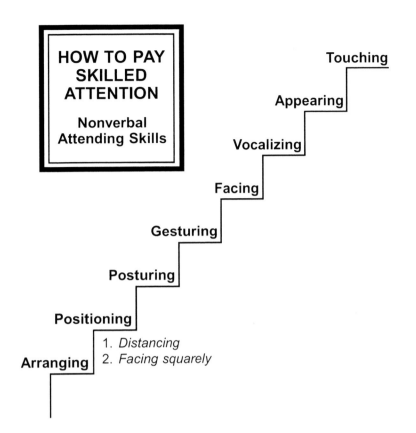

HOW TO PAY SKILLED ATTENTION

Nonverbal Attending Skills

Touching

Appearing

Vocalizing

Facing

Gesturing

Posturing

Positioning

1. *Distancing*
2. *Facing squarely*

Arranging

Positioning

Positioning means putting yourself in the best possible place to see and hear your partner. This helps you *see* and *hear* what is being communicated by your partner. The two sub-skills of Positioning are Distancing and Facing Squarely.

Physically positioning yourself in relation to your partner is very important in interacting with them. Although there are several different principles, or activities, that you may feel are important to effective positioning, we will focus on two basic parts of positioning: establishing an appropriate distance, and facing squarely with your partner.

As an effective partner, you need to position yourself where you can see and hear exactly what is being communicated. Being in a good position helps you to know just what's going on and, therefore, helps to resolve smaller issues before they become major problems. Positioning also communicates that you are interested in your partner, letting them know that they can feel secure because you care about their well-being.

Now let's look at the two positioning skills outlined above.

Positioning: Distancing

The first principle of distancing is to be able to observe and listen to what your partner is saying. Of course, there will be many situations where you can't see your partner (e.g., when you are talking on the phone) or listen to them (i.e., you can see their actions but can't hear what is being said).

But the majority of our interactions with our partners take place where we can both see and hear them. Imagine that your partner is talking with you in your kitchen. Choose a distance that enables you to observe and listen to them most effectively. We recommend a distance of 3 to 5 feet, if circumstances allow.

> **POSITIONING** means distancing yourself close enough to see and hear your partner while interacting with them.

DVD

POSITIONING: Distancing
— The *Wrong* Way and the *Right* Way

How to Be in a Personal Relationship

Practice

List two situations in which you think it would be a good idea to pay attention to the distance between you and your partner.

Example: When greeting each other at the end of the day.

1. _____

   _____

2. _____

   _____

Positioning: Facing Squarely

Facing squarely, or fully, ensures that your position allows you to pay the most effective and full attention. Your left shoulder should be lined up with your partner's right shoulder, and your right shoulder should be lined up with your partner's left shoulder. By facing squarely, you are communicating to your partner that they have your undivided attention. Both your head and body are in perfect alignment with your partner's.

> **POSITIONING** means facing your partner squarely.

Just as with distancing, facing squarely is not something you can always do because of the environment (e.g., riding in a car) or circumstances (e.g., with several friends and your partner). On the other hand, if it's an important issue that needs to be communicated with your partner, and the situation allows for it, you should position yourself for the most effective communication by distancing appropriately and facing squarely.

DVD

POSITIONING: Facing Squarely
 — The *Wrong* Way and the *Right* Way

Practice

List two situations in which you think it would be a good idea to face your partner squarely.

Example: When your partner asks you to listen to them.

1. _____

   _____

2. _____

   _____

Making the Point—The WRONG Way
The Case of the Talking Wall

Pat and Mark have been dating for three years, and they plan to marry next year. Mark has become increasingly annoyed with Pat regarding the way she talks to him when they are in the apartment together. He has decided that he needs to address it because it is literally driving him crazy.

Pat has a habit of yelling from one room to the other when she wants Mark's attention. Recently, we find Mark working at his computer on a project for work that required his undivided attention. He hears Pat yelling his name throughout the apartment. Mark decides not to respond and keeps working.

Suddenly, Pat comes to where Mark is working and asks him why he didn't acknowledge her. Mark responds, "If you had just come to where I was *(positioning)* you would see I was working, and I couldn't just jump up." Then he tells her that he thinks it's disrespectful for her to assume that what she wants is more important than what he may be doing. He asks her, as a courtesy, to come to where he is *(positioning)* before making requests of him.

How to Be in a Personal Relationship

Jessica and Juan have been married for six years. They would describe their relationship as very positive. About two years ago, they decided they would like to have children. So far, they haven't been successful, and it's been causing tension in their relationship.

Both Jessica and Juan decided to seek medical help. The results revealed that Juan has a medical condition that is the reason for their inability to conceive children. Juan received this news when the physician called him at work. Juan is very upset and decides to go home from work early so that he can collect his thoughts before talking with Jessica.

When Jessica arrives home, Juan hears her coming in the door. He immediately gets up from where he is sitting and greets her at the door. He takes her by the hand and asks her to sit across from him. He then tells her the news. After hearing Juan say everything he wanted to say, Jessica looks at Juan with a sympathetic look and tells him not to worry, they will work everything out together.

Action Strategies

Below are some Positioning Strategies you may want to use in your personal relationships if the situation allows for it.

1. You need your partner's help, but he/she is in another room.
    Go to the room he/she is in so that he/she can see you. Then make your request for help.

2. Your partner has just come in the door from work, and you hear them.
    Go to where your partner is, and say, "How was your day?"

3. Your partner has just come home from the grocery store and is carrying in some groceries. You are in the yard working.
    Stop what you are doing, walk toward your partner, and ask if he/she needs some help.

4. You are walking with your partner in the neighborhood.
    Walk by your partner's side rather than ahead or behind him/her.

5. Your partner is sitting on the couch in the den watching television. **Sit on the couch next to him/her rather than in the recliner you normally sit in.**

Now, write a Positioning Action Strategy:

_____

_____

_____

_____

_____

_____

How to Be in a Personal Relationship

Posturing

Using good posture means holding your body in a way that shows confidence, interest, and alertness. When you appear interested and alert, people will believe that you care. When you show confidence, you appear genuine in your caring. The two building blocks of Posturing are Standing/Sitting Erect and Leaning Forward.

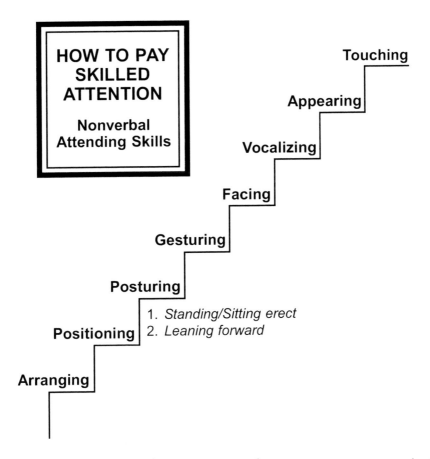

As with positioning, there are several ways you can use posturing when you are communicating with your partner. Here, we'll focus on two specific skills: Standing/Sitting Erect and Leaning Forward.

The way in which these two skills show confidence should be obvious. When you stand/ sit erect, you let people know that you are alert and in control of yourself. This lets them know you can manage anything they say without losing control of yourself.

Posturing: Standing/Sitting Erect

We all know how important erect posture is. You probably heard it as a child, and you definitely heard it if you were in the armed services: "Stand your full height," "Be proud," "Stand up straight," "Chin out," "Stick out that chest," and "Pull in that gut."

Erect posture takes muscle tone and practice. Look in the mirror and check yourself out. Are your shoulders straight? Is your chest caved in? How do you feel? Ask someone else for his or her reaction. Which way does he or she experience you as more confident and alert?

> **POSTURING** means standing/sitting erect to show confidence and alertness.

POSTURING: Sitting/Standing Erect
— The *Wrong* Way and the *Right* Way

Posturing: Leaning Forward

Your intention when you are leaning forward is to communicate interest and concern by shifting your weight so that people become more aware of your "inclination" to communicate with respect. Leaning forward sends a message that you are "moving closer" without physically moving you much closer or making any physical contact. Try leaning your weight *away* from another person. What do you experience? Probably a "laid-back" remoteness from the person. You are simply not as involved.

> **POSTURING** means leaning forward to show that you're really interested.

POSTURING: Leaning Forward
— The *Wrong* Way and the *Right* Way

How to Be in a Personal Relationship

Practice

List two situations where posturing is important in a personal relationship.

Example: Your partner is upset and needs to talk.

1. _____
   _____

2. _____
   _____

Making the Point—The WRONG Way
The Case of Bored Brad

Robin and Brad have been dating for a year. Robin likes Brad a lot, but something about the way he acts toward her is irritating her. When Robin wants to have a serious discussion about something, Brad has a habit of leaning back in his chair, his hands clasped behind his head. More often than not, he yawns while in this position.

Recently, Robin has decided she needs to talk with Brad about the concern she has regarding this habit. After all, Brad keeps asking Robin to move in with him. Robin is considering the move for a variety of reasons. They've talked about marriage. She lives alone and would like the security of living with someone she trusts. Her family lives in another state. It could also help with the finances. But can she live with the way he relates to her?

When Brad arrives at her apartment, she asks him to sit down. She tells him she would like to talk about living together. Immediately, Brad sits down, leans back on the couch, puts his feet on the coffee table, and places his hands behind his head. As he begins to yawn, Robin stands up and says angrily, "Obviously, you aren't taking this seriously," and storms out of the room.

Kim and Kyle have been dating for six months. Kim's parents are not happy about her dating Kyle. They don't believe Kyle is good enough for their daughter.

Kim is a college graduate, and now she is contemplating law school. Kyle is an auto mechanic who recently started his own business. Kyle's father died when he was 12, and Kyle has been on his own financially since he was 16. Kyle had the grades and would have liked to have gone to college, but it simply wasn't possible.

Recently, Kim got into a volatile disagreement with her parents over Kyle. They want her to break it off with him. She refused, and her father told her that he wouldn't support her while she went to law school as long as she was with Kyle.

Kim called Kyle and asked if they could meet. Kyle was always happy to get the chance to see Kim, so he went straight to her apartment. When he got to the apartment, Kim asked him to sit down. He took a seat in a chair directly across from Kim. He sat upright and leaned slightly toward her as she told him about the disagreement with her parents. Kyle never changed his sitting posture while Kim talked, even though some of what she said hurt him deeply.

After Kim told Kyle what had happened, Kyle told her that he was sorry the whole event had happened. Then he told her, without adjusting his posture, that he would understand if she wanted to break it off with him.

Kim responded, "No way! You know, one of the things that makes me so attracted to you is how you always seem to be able to stay calm yet confident— no matter what's going on. Thanks for always being there for me."

Kyle's dad had always told him to walk, stand, or sit up straight because it communicated strength. As Kyle left Kim's apartment that day, he looked up and thanked his dad again for a valuable lesson learned.

Action Strategies

Below are some Posturing Strategies you may want to use in your personal relationships if the situation allows for it.

1. You are having dinner with your partner in a restaurant. You are sitting directly across from him/her. You have both finished eating and your partner begins to talk about something that's important to him/her.

    Lean forward in your chair toward your partner as he/she begins to talk.

2. You are laying down on the sofa reading. Your partner enters the room obviously upset about something.

    Either stand up or sit up, holding your posture erect. Ask them to sit down next to you or across from you. Lean toward them as if they are directly across from you.

3. You are walking down the street. You see your partner approaching you. He/She seems excited. Your partner starts walking toward you, saying he/she has really good news.

    Start walking rapidly toward him/her. Stop when you get within 3 feet of your partner. Put your arms and hands down to your side. Square up with them. Your erect posture communicates alertness. Put your left foot slightly forward toward them, forcing your weight to shift slightly so that you are leaning in his/her direction. Then say, "What are you so excited about?"

4. Your spouse is looking a little down, sitting on the bed with his/her feet propped up and his/her head against the headboard. You ask your partner if he/she is okay. He/she says everything is all right, but the expression on your partner's face tells you otherwise.

    Sit down on the edge of the bed next to your partner with your feet on the floor. Turn your body to square directly with him/her. Keep your posture erect but with a slight lean toward your partner. Then say, "Are you sure? You don't look like you're okay. What's up?"

5. You are sitting on a blanket at the beach with your partner. You are about to share some food together.

   Turn your body toward your partner, your legs crossed in front of you. Keep your posture erect and lean slightly towards them.

Now, write a Posturing Action Strategy:

_____

_____

_____

_____

_____

_____

Gesturing

How you move your hands, arms, legs, or how you move in general can effect your social goals. Think about it: a finger pointed at you in a threatening manner probably makes you angry. Conversely, someone who is waving excitedly while saying, "Hello," probably makes you feel good.

The movement of our hands, arms, feet—even our head—can attract or detract from our social interactions. Unfortunately, most of us have gesturing behaviors that others find irritable but that we are unaware of. Gesturing sub-skills focus on eliminating gesturing behaviors that detract from our interactions and adding gesturing behaviors that others find attractive.

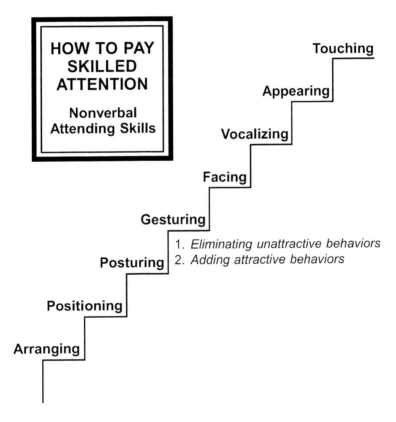

Gesturing is the ability to use movements of your hands, arms, legs and head that are attractive to another person while avoiding unattractive movements.

Gesturing: Eliminating Unattractive Behaviors

The first step in eliminating unattractive behaviors is becoming aware of gestures that others may find distracting or unattractive when they are talking with you. There are a lot of possibilities, but some of the most common are:

- Finger pointing
- Slamming fists down
- Waving your finger in disapproval
- Foot tapping
- Constant head nodding
- Finger tapping
- Fidgeting with keys, hair, glasses, etc.
- Grooming yourself
- Pacing while someone is talking
- Chewing gum/toothpicks
- Rolling your eyes
- Breaking eye contact
- Walking in front of a person while he/she is talking

GESTURING means eliminating behaviors that others might find distracting or unattractive when they are talking with you.

DVD

GESTURING: Eliminating Unattractive Behaviors — The *Wrong* Way and the *Right* Way

Practice

List three unattractive or distracting gestures that you may exhibit while talking.

1. _____

_____

2. _____

_____

3. _____

_____

How to Be in a Personal Relationship

List three unattractive or distracting gestures that people you care about have exhibited to you.

1. _____

   _____

2. _____

   _____

3. _____

   _____

Gesturing: Adding Attractive Behaviors

The second step in gesturing is to add movements that loved ones find attractive or inviting while you are talking with them. Some people believe keeping your body movements still while your partner is talking is better than making unattractive gestures. On the other hand, some people find *no* gesturing annoying because your lack of movement may imply neutrality or that you don't care. The key to attractive gesturing is knowing what most people find attractive and knowing when and where to apply it. For example, most people would find the following as attractive gesturing:

- Nodding one's head in approval
- Waving to someone
- Waving your arm and hand in a positive manner for them to come closer
- "Thumbs up" in approval
- Arms not crossed in front of chest
- Clasped hands in your lap while they are speaking
- Putting objects down (pens, paper, TV remote control, etc.)
- Open arms when you see them

> **GESTURING** means adding behaviors that others might find attractive or inviting when they are talking with you.

DVD

GESTURING: Adding Attractive Behaviors
— The *Wrong* Way and the *Right* Way

Practice

List three new attractive gestures that you would like to utilize when talking to a loved one.

1. _____

   _____

2. _____

   _____

3. _____

   _____

Making the Point—The WRONG Way
The Case of the Impatient Partner

Rosalind and Levon have been dating for about three months. Recently, Rosalind has noticed that Levon has specific gestures that he exhibits when he is irritated. If they are walking together when he gets irritated, he tends to walk in front of her, and he keeps increasing the distance as they keep walking. Then he turns toward her and raises his arm and hand in a way that implies she needs to hurry up. He also has a tendency to begin pacing in front of her while she is getting ready to go out with him.

Recently, she noticed that when she tells him she doesn't want to do something he wants to do, he begins tapping his foot and cracking his knuckles.

Rosalind is concerned that these gestures may indicate that he might get worse with time, possibly indicating that he will lose his temper with her.

How to Be in a Personal Relationship

Making the Point—The RIGHT Way
The Case of the Purse Retriever

Gloria and Jake have been dating for about a year. Recently, while at dinner with friends, Gloria tells Jake that she left her purse in his car and asks him if he would mind getting it for her.

Jake smiles and slowly moves his chair back from behind the table. As he stands, Gloria says, "Sorry." Jake smiles and says, with palms open, "No problem," winks and proceeds out to the car.

Upon returning with Gloria's purse, he hands it to Gloria, smiles, and touches her on the shoulder. He then returns to his seat. As he begins to sit, Gloria gives him a look of appreciation. Jake responds with a hand gesture implying that it's no big deal.

Action Strategies

Below are some Gesturing Strategies you may want to use in your personal relationships if the situation allows for it.

1. Your partner has just received a phone call that has upset them. They approach you to discuss it. You are sitting at a desk doing paperwork.

    Pull up a chair so that it is directly in front of you, and ask your partner to sit down. As he/she talks to you, keep your body (gesturing) completely still, and say nothing until he/she has finished telling you about the phone call.

2. You are meeting your partner for dinner at a restaurant and have arrived earlier than him/her. You see your partner pull in to the parking lot.

    Immediately wave to your partner as if you are excited to see him/her.

3. You are sitting across the table from your partner having dinner. He/she begins to tell you about an event at work that made him/her feel good.

    As your partner begins to describe it, look directly at him/her, occasionally nodding your head, acknowledging his/her excitement over what happened.

4. You are walking with your partner and suddenly realize you have gotten ahead of him/her.

    Look back and notice. Stop. Then extend your arm out, gesturing for them to come on. Your gesture is a patient one, implying that he/she is not holding you up.

5. Your partner is performing in an event (e.g., singing in the church choir, acting in a play, participating in an athletic event). He/she spots you in the audience.

    Give him/her a "thumbs up" gesture of approval.

Now, write a Gesturing Action Strategy:

_____

_____

_____

_____

_____

_____

Facing

Facing is the ability to communicate through facial expression. The face of another person is often the first thing we look at when we encounter them. The use of facial expressions is often seen as the most powerful aspect of nonverbal attending.

The face is considered a direct link to the emotional state of a person. If a person's face reflects a negative emotion such as anger, fear, or sadness, it can directly affect another person's reaction to them. Conversely, a facial expression of happiness or empathy can generate a positive reaction from the person viewing it. The two skills involved in Facing are establishing and maintaining appropriate eye contact and managing your facial expression.

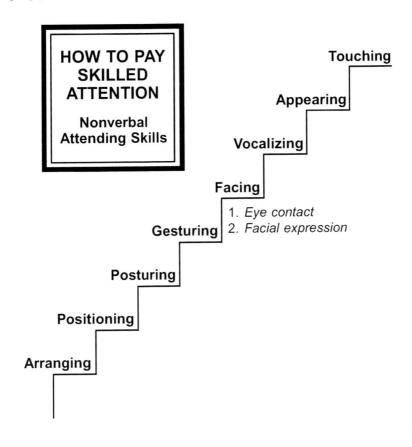

HOW TO PAY SKILLED ATTENTION

Nonverbal Attending Skills

Touching

Appearing

Vocalizing

Facing
1. *Eye contact*
2. *Facial expression*

Gesturing

Posturing

Positioning

Arranging

Facing: Eye Contact

Appropriate eye contact may be the best way of communicating interest. People become aware of our efforts to make contact with them when they see us looking directly at their faces. Of course, looking directly at people will also provide you with valuable information about them. For example, people who keep shifting their eyes while talking to you signal that, at the very least, they are either uncomfortable with you or with what is being said. This kind of information is important in sizing up a person's mood or emotional state.

In addition to the information you can get by observing others, appropriate eye contact tells people that you are confident and not threatened. Although appropriate eye contact doesn't mean you should get involved in a staring contest, many people believe that a person who won't look you in the eyes may be afraid of disclosing something to you.

You must keep in mind that "direct" eye contact may be threatening to some people based on the individual's past experiences, the individual's cultural and/or societal rules, and/or the circumstances surrounding your current conversation.

FACING means establishing and maintaining
appropriate eye contact.

DVD

FACING: Eye Contact
— The *Wrong* Way and the *Right* Way

Practice

List two circumstances where eye contact may be inappropriate.

Example: Person you're looking at is angry.

1. _____

   _____

2. _____

   _____

How to Be in a Personal Relationship

List two circumstances where eye contact is appropriate.

Example: Person you're looking at is upset.

1. _____

_____

2. _____

_____

Facing: Facial Expression

The human face is capable of many expressions too numerous to list or practice. Many of us are unaware of our facial expressions because it is difficult to see our own expressions. A good rule of thumb is to realize that our emotional state (angry, scared, sad, happy, etc.) is frequently reflected in our facial display.

Some cultures stress "facial display rules." The purpose of these rules is to make sure that a person's "facial displays" (i.e., expressions) do not accurately reveal the person's true emotional state. These display rules are often taught as a form of social etiquette.

On the other hand, a lack of facial expression can create problems. Many of us feel uneasy with people who show very little or no expression in their face (**Hint:** Think of someone who always seems to show a "poker face"). The reason for our discomfort is that most of us want to be able to look at another person's face to see if the words they are saying match their expression. When there is a match, we may feel the person is more sincere or trustworthy. When the expression and words don't match, we tend to get a "gut feeling" that something is wrong, and we may become suspicious of the person.

The important issue to keep in mind is that our facial expressions need to be conveyed, yet managed, depending on our social goal. For example, if you are angry at someone and they are angry at you, exercising control of your facial display of anger can be critical in lowering the anger in yourself *as well as in the other person.*

Conversely, maintaining a facial expression of concern or empathy for a loved one who is upset, even when you are tired, has a lot of social benefit. Keep in mind that we are not suggesting you be fraudulent in your facial displays. We are, however, suggesting that you learn to regulate those displays, especially during critical interactions between you and a loved one.

> **FACING** means that your facial expressions need
> to be conveyed, yet managed, depending
> on your social goal.

DVD

FACING: Facial Expression
— The *Wrong* Way and the *Right* Way

Practice

List two common negative facial expressions you probably exhibit, when you exhibit them, and the facial expression you convey.

Example: I look *angry* when my partner and I discuss money, and I would like to convey *neutrality* until all the facts are on the table.

1. _____

   _____

2. _____

   _____

Making the Point—The WRONG Way
The Case of Two Wrongs Being Plain Wrong

Steffie and Jon have been married for almost five years. Recently, Jon has noticed that when Steffie comes home from work, her facial expression is one of great irritation. Steffie is unhappy in her current job, but doesn't want to leave it because she doesn't like change. Steffie will wear this facial expression, often through dinner, no matter what Jon says to cheer her up.

Out of frustration, Jon decides to confront Steffie about this one evening after dinner. Jon is angry when he decides to confront Steffie, and this is reflected in *his* facial expression. As Jon begins to tell Steffie about his frustration, she becomes upset. Jon continues to express his anger and frustration (in his mind, patiently) when Steffie gets up and says, "I've had it," and retreats to the bedroom, locking the door behind her.

Jon spent the night on the living room sofa. Steffie rarely spoke to Jon for the next two evenings, and when she did, it was either negative or cold in both facial and voice tone.

How to Be in a Personal Relationship

Beverly and Carlos have been married 15 years. They have three children and describe their marriage as a solid one. Five years ago, Beverly was diagnosed with breast cancer. Her prognosis at the time was not good—the doctors didn't expect Beverly to live more than two years. Before the cancer, Beverly had always been described as an "up" person by her friends. That didn't change throughout her diagnosis and treatment. And now here she was, five years later—alive and in remission.

Recently, Carlos came home from his job at the automobile plant. He had just heard that there were going to be layoffs at the plant. He was obviously down as he entered the house, but he didn't want to say anything to Beverly because her cancer treatments had put them in financial jeopardy, and they were just coming out of it.

But Beverly was one of those people from whom it was difficult to hide things. She would look directly at you while speaking to you. Today was no different, and when she greeted Carlos at the door, she could see the look of fear on his face. She asked him what was wrong, to which he said, "Nothing."

Not willing to let it go, Beverly told Carlos that he needed to be straight with her if something was wrong. The look on her face was one of confidence and understanding, and Carlos knew he would have to level with her. Finally, Carlos relented. He told her about the layoffs. Beverly looked at him with her typical sheepish grin and said everything would be just fine. After all, they had each other.

Action Strategies

Below are some Facing Strategies you may want to use in your personal relationships if the situation allows for it.

1. Your partner has just arrived home. You are outside when he/she drives up.

    Walk toward him/her. Look directly into your partner's face and eyes. Say, "Hi! How are you?" while continuing to look at him/her.

2. The next time your partner is talking with you about something that concerns him/her...

    Maintain a facial expression of concern while he/she is talking. (*Hint:* One of the best ways to maintain facial expressions is to *feel* the emotion inside *yourself*. If you *feel* concern, the face will often cooperate).

3. While at a social gathering (e.g., party, dinner with friends, etc.), when you spot your partner,

    Look directly at your partner when he/she sees you. You may want to give him/her a wink and a smile.

4. While talking to your partner, you notice they can't look at you (*Hint:* Often when people are sad, they can't look at others). If you are in close proximity to your partner,

    Gently put your hand under your partner's chin and gradually lift his/her face so that he/she can look at you. Then look directly at your partner and gently smile.

5. Your partner is angry at you about something. You are standing across the room from your partner while he/she is expressing his/her feelings.

    Look at your partner, without an angry expression on your face. When you get eye contact with your partner, try to give a facial expression of concern/empathy (*Hint:* Keep in mind that when a person is angry at you, and you look at them with an angry expression, it can increase their anger toward you).

Now, write a Facing Action Strategy:

_____

_____

_____

_____

_____

_____

Vocalizing

Teaching someone to be aware of his/her voice volume and tone is just as difficult as teaching someone to be aware of his/her facial expressions. Despite this, learning to control the way you vocalize is critical. Our voice volume and tone, just like facial expressions, are directly linked to our emotional states. Consequently, if our voice tone conveys anger, anxiety, sadness, or happiness, it can directly affect the emotional state of the other person with whom we are talking. For example, if you are angry at your partner, but don't want to display anger in your words, your voice tone will often "give you away," clearly communicating the anger.

It's important to keep in mind that regulating your emotions can be critical in stressful situations. All too often, people believe that they have a right to their feelings and should express their true emotions. Of course, there are times when this is true, and there are other times when regulating your emotions will be the more intelligent thing to do. We will be talking about this in more depth in Section II of the book, Emotion Management.

We will be examining two sub-skills of Vocalizing: Managing the Volume of your voice, and Managing the Tone of your voice.

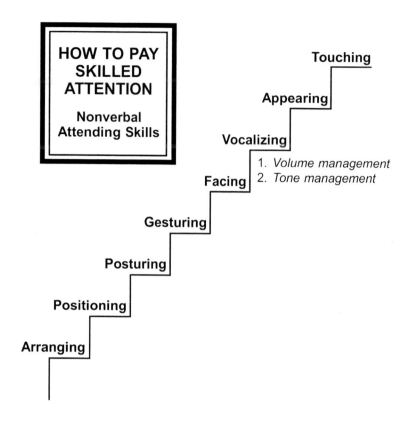

HOW TO PAY SKILLED ATTENTION

Nonverbal Attending Skills

Touching

Appearing

Vocalizing
1. *Volume management*
2. *Tone management*

Facing

Gesturing

Posturing

Positioning

Arranging

Vocalizing: Volume Management

The volume of one's voice is measured by terms such as *loudness* and *softness*. It is important because it affects another person's ability to hear you. For example, when you turn up the volume on your stereo, it is because you are unable to hear it to comprehend the words. On the other hand, if it's too loud, you turn it down so that you can hear the words. The key to volume is finding one that is not too loud and not too low so that you can ensure that others can hear and comprehend your words.

Occasionally, there may be some circumstances during which your voice volume might have to be raised to overcome competing sounds. For example, you may find yourself raising your voice volume if you and your partner are in a crowded area and become separated.

Conversely, when you are in close proximity to your partner, you may want to lower your volume. For example, when you are sitting next to each other at the breakfast table or riding in the car together, you are more likely to use a lower volume to communicate.

The goal to volume management is to be aware of it and to utilize it based on the social circumstance you are in with your partner.

> **VOCALIZING** means managing your volume so that it is neither too high nor too low, and can be comprehended by others with whom you are interacting.

DVD

> **VOCALIZING: Adding Attractors**
> **— The *Wrong* Way and the *Right* Way**

Practice

List two situations where you would want to regulate your *volume* when speaking to a loved one.

Example: When he/she is very ill and in a hospital room.

1. _____

   _____

2. _____

   _____

Vocalizing: Tone Management

The difference between volume and tone is that voice tone is a more accurate and focused reflection of your emotional state than voice volume. When someone says they heard an angry or sad tone in another person's voice, they are referring to the emotions that the speaker is experiencing and how those emotions are being conveyed through their voice tone. Remember, we are talking about nonverbal skills for now, so we aren't referring to the *words* the speaker may be using to describe their emotion, but to the tone of voice that accompanies the words.

Have you ever thought someone had a "bad attitude" simply because of the *way* they said something, but not so much from the words they used? If so, the tone of their voice was probably one thing that contributed to that impression (along with other indicators, such as a facial display of "disgust"). Our voice tone is often a direct reflection, or link, to our inner emotions, and because of that, regulating our voice tone can be difficult. But just like our facial expressions, our tone of voice needs to be regulated so that social goals can be met in a constructive manner. For instance, if your partner says to you they love you in a loving tone, and you respond back, "I love you, too," in a cold or detached tone, it can change the course of your interaction quickly.

> **VOCALIZING** means understanding that your tone
> of voice is a direct link to your inner emotions,
> and that tone must be regulated so that social goals
> can be met in a constructive manner.

DVD

VOCALIZING: Tone Management
— The *Wrong* Way and the *Right* Way

Practice

List two situations where you would want to regulate your voice tone when speaking to a loved one. **Example:** You are upset with your partner based on something you heard from someone else, but you don't have all the facts.

1. _____

   _____

2. _____

   _____

Making the Point—The WRONG Way
The Case of Catching More Flies with
Honey than Vinegar

Alicia and Tyrone have been married for about three years. They have no children, and both of them have demanding jobs. Recently, Alicia has been frustrated with Tyrone's lack of help around the house. Every night she brings it up, and every night Tyrone says he'll help—but not tonight. Finally, Alicia has decided that she has had enough of Tyrone's lack of follow-through. She is going to confront him in no uncertain terms when he gets home from work.

As Tyrone comes in from work around 8:00 p.m. (he works a lot of overtime and leaves the house around 6:00 a.m.), Alicia tells him, in a very angry tone, "I've had it!" Upon hearing this, Tyrone turns around, shuts the door behind him, and goes to his brother's house to spend the night.

The next day, Alicia has calmed down and calls Tyrone at work to apologize.

(continued)

How to Be in a Personal Relationship

(concluded)

That night, when Tyrone comes in from work, he tells her he appreciated her call. He then says, "Look, the reason I haven't been helping when you asked was because you always have this 'tone' in your voice when you ask me for help. I get the feeling that you're practically accusing me of not doing anything to contribute to the household. Last night, when you got angry, I'd had enough."

He went on to remind her that he works the extra overtime because she asked him to since they needed extra money for the car payment on her new car. He added, "Honey, I don't mind doing things for you—for us—but it would really help me feel valued if I didn't hear the sarcasm in your voice every time you ask for help."

Making the Point—The RIGHT Way
The Case of the Voice of Reason

Nancy and Alan have been married for six years. Recently, Alan's friend, Sam, told him that "he didn't want Alan to take it the wrong way, but Nancy has the neatest sounding voice he's ever heard." Sam has never met Nancy. Alan started to laugh and told him the story about why he decided to ask Nancy to marry him.

It seems that Nancy and he had been dating for about six months. He got angry at Nancy about something and proceeded to let her know. While he was talking, Nancy simply remained quiet. When he finished, Nancy looked at him, began to grin, and said, "I like it when you get mad. You're so cute." For Alan, it wasn't just *what* she had said, but the *way* she had said it—in the most genuine, non-angry tone. He was wowed by her from that point on. Since then, he added, Nancy had showed him that she had the ability to maintain the most positive tone of voice no matter what words she used.

Action Strategies

Below are some Vocalizing Strategies you may want to use in your personal relationships if the situation allows for it.

1.   Your partner raises his/her voice at you because he/she is angry.
     Respond back using a non-angry tone and moderate volume level (keep in mind that this is difficult to do without practice).

2. Your partner is having difficulty hearing you in a mall where there is a lot of noise distraction.

    Raise the volume of your voice to a level he/she can hear you, but not so loud that your partner thinks you are yelling at him/her.

3. You are on the phone with your partner. He/She is talking with you about a problem he/she is having. Your partner sounds upset. When it's your turn to respond to him/her:

    Use a caring tone of voice throughout the conversation.

4. You haven't seen your partner for a couple of days. When you come into your residence, your partner smiles and says, "Hello! I missed you!"

    Tell your partner that you missed him/her, too, using a loving tone.

5. You are angry with your partner about something he/she said on the phone earlier in the day. When you get home, you are still angry about it, and you want to talk to him/her about it. You decide to wait until after dinner. After dinner, you sit down in the living room. As you begin to tell your partner about your anger, you find yourself becoming angry inside. You also notice your voice volume is increasing.

    Stop and pause for a few seconds. Start over again using a non-angry tone, but a firm tone, and keep your voice volume low.

Now, write a Vocalizing Action Strategy:

_____

_____

_____

_____

_____

_____

Appearing

A person's appearance is an important indicator about how a person wants to be seen by others. There are those who think it is the most important factor in their communication with others, and there are those who think that physical appearance shouldn't matter at all. There is no doubt that one's physical appearance affects the way others see them. Research shows that we are drawn to people who are physically attractive. However, it is a misguided belief to think that physical attraction is sufficient enough to maintain a long-term relationship. The reality is that physical appearance matters as much as all of the other nonverbal communicators we have discussed to this point when it comes to influencing social outcomes.

In this section, our intent is to emphasize the maintenance of a positive physical appearance as a nonverbal indicator about how a person feels about his/her relationship. Now, we aren't concentrating so much about the elements of appearance about which we have no control (e.g., the effects of disease, aging, genetics, etc.). Instead, we want to emphasize the physical appearance factors that one has control over and/or can maintain. In other words, we want to speak to the physical appearance issues that can be measured by grooming and hygiene—action strategies a person is able to perform to maintain their optimal appearance.

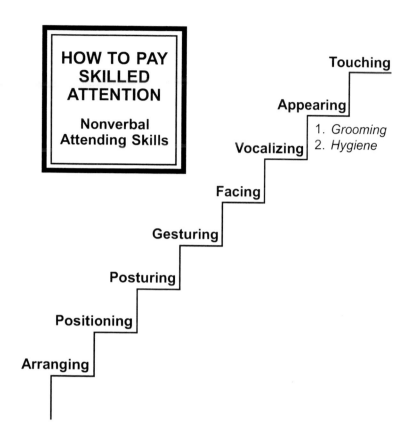

Appearing: Grooming

Grooming is the ability to take care of your physical appearance through the use of dressing, brushing, and primping action strategies. Dressing strategies refer to the selecting, maintaining, and wearing of clothes based on the occasion and circumstances. Brushing strategies refer to the maintenance of one's body hair. This refers to shaving, combing, removing, coloring, or styling of ones body hair. Primping strategies refer to wearing make-up, maintaining skin, maintaining finger- and toenails, controlling body odor, and wearing cologne or perfume.

> **APPEARING** means *making use of grooming strategies* such as dressing, brushing, and primping to optimize your physical appearance.

APPEARING: Grooming
— The *Wrong* Way and the *Right* Way

Practice

List two specific grooming strategies that are important to a personal relationship.

Example: On the mornings I do not have to attend work, I get up, shave, comb my hair, and dress in clean casual clothing before having breakfast with my partner.

1. _____

_____

2. _____

_____

Appearing: Hygiene

Hygiene is the ability to maintain the health of your body and physical being. This involves cleaning, eating right (nutrition), exercising, and accessing appropriate medical care action strategies. Cleaning strategies include cleaning of skin, hair, teeth, nails, and other body parts. Nutrition strategies involve proper food intake. Exercise strategies involve muscle maintenance, cardio-respiratory fitness, ligament and tendon flexibility, and static and dynamic strength. Medical strategies involve regular physicals, weight control, physical health monitoring, and preventive health measures.

> **APPEARING** means *making use of hygiene strategies* such as cleaning, eating right (nutrition), exercising, and accessing appropriate medical care to optimize your physical appearance.

DVD

APPEARING: Hygiene
— The *Wrong* Way and the *Right* Way

Practice

List two specific hygiene action strategies that are important to a personal relationship.

Example: Prior to going to bed with my partner, I take a shower, brush and floss my teeth, and shave.

1. _____

_____

2. _____

_____

Making the Point—The WRONG Way
The Case of the Caveman

Janice and Joshua have been married for ten years. They met during Janice's sophomore year in college, and Janice thought Joshua was in great physical condition.

When they married following their graduation from college, Joshua was jogging several days per week and maintaining his physical appearance. He was also concerned about his grooming. He combed his hair, regularly brushed his teeth, and sometimes showered twice a day.

About four years ago, Joshua's appearance started to change. He went from a 34-inch waistline to a 40-inch waistline, gaining about 60 pounds seemingly overnight. During the week, Joshua would shower and shave every morning before going to work. Weekends, however, were different—Joshua wouldn't shower or shave until Sunday evening. He told Janice that weekends were his time to unwind and do as he pleased. Recently, Joshua had complained about Janice's unwillingness to have sexual contact with him. As a matter of fact, they were only sexually active once a month on average—and that encounter was brief.

Now Joshua has become frustrated with his lack of sexual contact with Janice, and he has confronted her about it. Janice angrily responds, "You have got to be kidding! I am sick of being married to a caveman. Your breath is bad, your teeth are turning yellow, and. . . **you stink**. Especially on the weekends! Since when did using deodorant become an option?" Joshua was angry and shocked. They haven't spoken for two weeks, and nothing's changed.

How to Be in a Personal Relationship

Chanda and Jason have been married for 25 years. They have three children; two have graduated from college, and their youngest child is entering his first year of college.

Recently, Chanda and Jason were at a high school reunion. Jason was talking with several of his former high school friends, and one said, "Jason, I don't know how you two do it." Jason responded, "Do what?" The friend said, "You both look great! Chanda looks like she could be your daughter. I remember her in high school, and she was attractive then, but she looks like she's hardly aged. You're lucky." Jason just smiled and responded, "I know."

That evening, while driving home from the reunion, Jason looked over at Chanda and said, "You're incredible." He then told Chanda about the compliments from his friends. Chanda responded, "It's easy—I've got you." She added, "I try to take care of myself because it's important to me, but I also do it out of respect for our relationship."

Action Strategies

Below are some Appearing Strategies you may want to use in your personal relationships if the situation allows for it.

1. Every morning, walk 2 miles before getting ready for work.

2. Every day, brush your teeth, comb your hair, and dress in clean clothes—even on weekends.

3. Do not go to bed in hair curlers, facial masks, or facial creams.

4. Maintain normal positive hygiene habits of brushing your teeth, bathing, and shaving—even when you don't feel well (e.g., cold, flu, etc.).

5. Dress in a fashion that's appropriate for you as well as to the circumstances and to your partner's expectations.

Now, write an Appearing Action Strategy:

_____

_____

_____

_____

_____

_____

Touching

Touch is one of the most powerful nonverbal communicators. If done appropriately, it can have significant positive results. If done inappropriately, it can cause significant *negative* results. Most of us are not formally taught about how to touch another person. As a matter of fact, most of our touching behaviors are learned by watching others over the course of our daily lives or by trial-and-error. Consequently, either we tend to not touch or we run the risk of touching inappropriately.

How we touch is often determined by the nature of the relationship. For example, how a father hugs his infant daughter will change as his daughter grows into maturity. Conversely, how a mother hugs her son as an infant will change as he grows into maturity.

There are also cultural differences that dictate what is "appropriate touch." In some cultures, men hold hands with other men not unlike the way women may hold hands in American culture. In some cultures, rubbing noses is a way to greet another person. In another culture, a kiss on each cheek is the norm.

The meaning, or intent, of a touch also shapes the communication or message. A friendly kiss is different than an intimate kiss. A massage therapist's touch has different meaning than the touch of your lover's hands.

The situations or circumstances that are in effect when the touch is made are another factor that influences the interpretation of the touch. The hugging between a group of athletes during a victory celebration in the locker room differs from hugs given in a private setting after the game.

We cannot address all the factors involved in touch. We cannot elaborate on all the different types of touch, just as we could not address all the different types of facial expressions and tones of voice a person is capable of. For the sake of this book, touch will be addressed as it relates to a personal relationship between adults, and we will consider three aspects of Touching: When to touch, Where to touch, and How to touch.

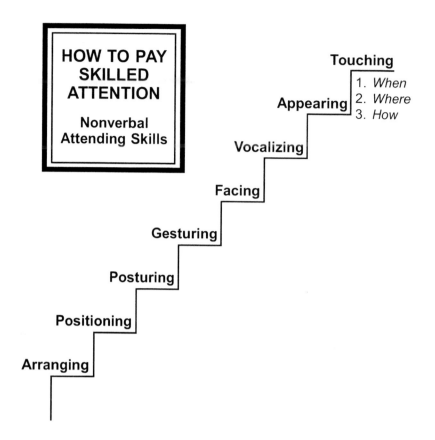

HOW TO PAY SKILLED ATTENTION

Nonverbal Attending Skills

Touching
1. *When*
2. *Where*
3. *How*

Appearing

Vocalizing

Facing

Gesturing

Posturing

Positioning

Arranging

Touching: When

The timing of touch is important when emotions are involved. For example, if someone is angry at you, they may not want to be touched. On the other hand, if they are sad, they may need the comfort of being touched.

Timing is also important in terms of when you touch a person during a conversation. For instance, imagine that you are talking with your partner while sitting directly across from them. They are initially very talkative, but as the conversation continues, they get quiet. At this point, you may elect to reach across and put your hand on top of theirs as a powerful way of inviting them to talk.

> **TOUCHING** means knowing *when* to touch
> another person appropriately.

TOUCHING: When
— The *Wrong* Way and the *Right* Way

Practice

List an example of the right time to touch and the wrong time to touch.

1. Right: _____

   _____

2. Wrong: _____

   _____

Touching: Where

The environment, or physical space, you are in is critical in making a decision to touch someone. For example, an intimate kiss with your partner may be inappropriate in a public place versus that same kiss in the privacy of your residence.

The environment also refers to the presence of other people in your physical space and the nature of their relationship to you. For instance, the above "intimate" kiss in front of your partner's parents may not be appropriate. Conversely, a "friendly" kiss or hug in front of those same parents may be very appropriate.

> **TOUCHING** means knowing *where*, or *in what environment*, it's appropriate to touch another person.

TOUCHING: Where
— The *Wrong* Way and the *Right* Way

Practice

List an example of where it would be appropriate (i.e., environment and people present) to touch intimately and where it would be inappropriate (i.e., environment and people present) to touch intimately.

1. Appropriate: _____

_____

2. Inappropriate: _____

_____

Touching: How

In this section, *how* really refers to the type of touch. By type, we are referring to things like a kiss, hug, hand touch, toe touch, etc. Type also refers to where you touch the other person on their body. A kiss on the lips is different than a kiss on the cheek. A hug that is cheek-to-cheek is different than a hug where your arms are wrapped around each other's waist. A hand touch on the shoulder is different than a hand touch on the lower back.

Type also refers to the meaning of the touch. Obviously, meaning should be controlled by the nature of the relationship. A kiss between friends is different than a kiss between lovers—a kiss between friends is going to be brief, whereas a kiss between lovers is going to be long.

> **TOUCHING** means knowing *how* to touch by understanding what type of touch is appropriate and the meaning that the touch conveys.

DVD

TOUCHING: How
— The *Wrong* Way and the *Right* Way

How to Be in a Personal Relationship

Practice

List two examples of how to touch someone based on the nature of the relationship.

Example: Embrace your partner for several seconds in a public place (airport) after having not seen them for a while or if you are not going to see them for a while.

1. _____

   _____

2. _____

   _____

Making the Point—The WRONG Way
The Case of the Ex-Boyfriend

Danielle and Stuart have been dating for several months. Not long ago, they were out together having dinner, and a former boyfriend of Danielle's was in the same restaurant. The ex-boyfriend approached them and introduced himself to Stuart. After the ex-boyfriend walked away, Stuart said something to Danielle that started an argument between them.

The argument escalated in the car after Danielle and Stuart left the restaurant. Stuart made another comment about the ex-boyfriend regarding how intimate Danielle and the ex-boyfriend had been. Danielle became more upset and, out of anger, told Stuart it was none of his business. After that, they both became silent for the duration of the drive back to Danielle's apartment.

They've just arrived at Danielle's apartment, and now Stuart is feeling bad about the things he said and about getting angry. As Danielle proceeds to get out of the car, Stuart attempts to put his arm around her, and kiss Danielle good night. She pushes his hand away and gets out of the car, slamming the door behind her. Now Stuart is angry again and drives off.

Su Li and Timothy have been married for 15 years. They have two children, ages eight and ten. Su Li has just come home from her annual physical. She had noticed a lump in her breast area earlier in the week and was hoping the physical would alleviate her fears, but the physician seemed concerned and suggested that Su Li get a mammogram as soon as possible.

Timothy sees Su Li coming in the door. He was aware of Su Li's concerns regarding the lump, and he is anxious to hear what the doctor said. As Su Li tells Timothy about the physician's concern and the mammogram, Timothy asks her to take a seat. He sits directly across from her and looks directly at her with a facial expression of concern. He lets Su Li talk and, after letting her talk for several minutes, he takes her hands into his and simply holds them.

Later that evening, as they are lying in bed together, Timothy puts his arms around Su Li and holds her until she falls asleep.

Action Strategies

Below are some Touching Strategies you may want to use in your personal relationships if the situation allows for it.

1. You are riding in the car with your partner. You are reading and he/she is driving.

    Reach over and put your hand on your partner's shoulder.

2. You walk up behind your partner in the kitchen. He/she is cleaning up, and you have come in to help.

    Put your hands on your partner's shoulders, kiss him/her on the back of the head, and then begin to help him/her clean up.

3. You are sitting on the sofa with your partner who is laying down reading a book while you watch television.

    Reach over and lift his/her feet into your lap. Begin to rub your partner's feet gently while you continue to watch television.

4. You are watching your partner on the telephone. He/She is obviously having a discussion with someone that appears to be stressing him/her.

    Walk up behind your partner, put your arms around his/her waist, and kiss him/her on the back of their head; then walk away without saying anything.

5. You are walking with your partner. He/She is talking about his/her day at work.

    Stop, grab his/her hand, look directly at your partner, pull him/her toward you, and begin to hug your partner while saying how much you appreciate him/her.

Now, write a Touching Action Strategy:

_____

_____

_____

_____

_____

_____

Skills Summary
Nonverbal Attending Skills

Now let's review all of the skills and sub-skills involved in Nonverbal Attending.

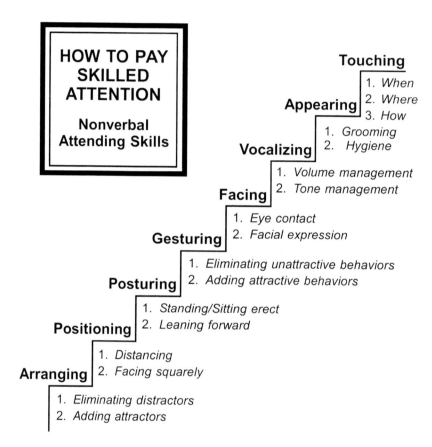

Chapter 2
Mental Attending

Mental attending occurs when you are able to focus your senses *and your thoughts* on the person you are attending to. Previously, we discussed the importance of your senses as it relates to being aware of the world around you. The key word here is *aware*. Our senses are the mechanisms nature has given us to be aware of the people, things, and events in our environment.

The opposite of being aware is to be ignorant. In other words, we **ignore**, or do not pay attention to, our surroundings. So when our partner accuses us of being insensitive to his/her needs or the needs of the relationship, he/she may really be saying we are not aware of those needs, *or* we are ignoring them.

The more aware you become of your environment, the less mistakes you will make regarding that environment. For example, a failure to notice the things that your partner contributes to your relationship (e.g., washing clothes, paying bills, cleaning the home, maintaining employment and income, etc.) implies that you are not aware of how important your partner's presence is in your life. See if the following "Making the Points" sound familiar.

Making the Point—The WRONG Way
The Case of the Man in the Mirror

Barry is currently moving into an apartment. He and his wife, Nikita, recently separated after 12 years of marriage. As he moved into the apartment, he is feeling very uneasy. This is the first time he has lived alone. It is also the first time he will not be living in the same house as his children.

Nikita had been telling Barry that there were problems in their relationship for several years. He had ignored her, assuming it was the normal growth pains all relationships go through. He couldn't believe it when his wife recently told him she was no longer in love with him and needed some space. She said she cared about him and wanted their divorce to be amicable.

Barry could not sleep his first night in the apartment. He kept trying to think of what he had done wrong. He believed he had done everything right. He had worked hard to get the several job promotions he had achieved. They had a nice home. He thought he was a good parent. Eventually, his thoughts drifted to

(continued)

other conversations in their marriage. Nikita kept telling him the past few years that he was never home, and she felt like a single parent. She added that they had been sleeping in separate beds for over two years. At first, Nikita had said it was due to Barry's snoring. Later, she said she was no longer physically attracted to him because of his significant weight gain.

As he got up to get a drink of water, he decided to look at a picture of his wife and daughters in his wallet. As he looked through the wallet, he noticed a picture of himself and his wife that had been taken while they were dating. As he looked at the photograph, he stepped into the bathroom. He looked at the picture and then at himself in the mirror. He was shocked. Nikita was right—not only had he failed to pay attention to his marriage, he hadn't been paying attention to himself. Looking at the man in the mirror, he wondered where the man in the photograph had gone.

Making the Point—The RIGHT Way
The Case of Fletcher's Follow-up

Evandra and Fletcher have been married for eight years. Evandra is a very outgoing person. She engages people easily, she smiles a lot, and she never seems to be at a loss for words.

Evandra has always taken pride in her appearance. Even on weekends or her off days from work, she will get up, comb her hair, and dress in neat, casual clothing—unless she is going to the gym to work out. When she goes to the gym, she wears stylish workout clothes, pulls her hair back, and wears some light makeup.

About four weeks ago, Evandra came home from work and made a negative comment about her new boss. When Fletcher asked her what was wrong, she responded that she could handle it. Since then, Evandra has been coming home from work later than usual. In the past, she has worked overtime periodically, but now it is an every night occurrence.

Over the past two weeks, Fletcher has noticed that Evandra has been quieter than is normal for her. Although she still smiles when she sees him, it is different somehow. He's also noticed that Evandra has not gone to the gym the past two weekends, and she's staying in her pajamas and bathrobe until around noon on her off days. Based on these observations, Fletcher decides he needs to start paying closer attention to Evandra over the next couple of days.

It is now Wednesday night, and Evandra has come home late again—around 7:00 p.m. Fletcher has prepared her favorite meal for her, hoping to surprise

(continued)

---

her. Evandra acknowledges Fletcher and tells him she appreciates his going to the trouble to make the meal, but she eats very little of it. Soon, she says she is tired and would like to go to bed early tonight.

Fletcher decides it is time to start asking Evandra some questions about what's wrong. He starts by sharing with her all of the changes in her behaviors and appearance he has noticed lately. He also comments that these changes seem to have occurred since her new boss arrived. While he talks with Evandra, he provides her with his undivided attention, using his nonverbal attending skills.

Initially, Evandra is reluctant to say anything. She then says, "Fletcher, I need to tell you something that is going on at work, and I don't know what to do about it." She continues, "The new boss I have at work is Jack Smith, the son of Douglas Smith. You know him, he's the owner of the company. Well, Jack has been asking me to work lots of overtime lately. He seems to set it up where I'm the only one working. Well, he's been making comments about how nice I look, and last week, he came up behind me and put his hands on my waist. When I told him to stop, he did, but he made a comment about my job security."

While Evandra has been telling the story to Fletcher, he has remained calm using good nonverbal and mental attending skills.

Evandra continues to share with Fletcher saying, "I've been scared to tell you because I love you, and I used to love my job, too—at least until now. And I know we need the money to pay off our school debts. Honey, I can't tell you how much it means to me that you are staying so calm and listening to me. I just don't know what to do. This guy gives me the creeps, even though he really hasn't done anything extreme.

Fletcher remains calm and says, "I don't care about the money. I don't want you putting up with that situation any more. I want you to quit. It's not worth it. I would like to have a talk with him myself, but I know it would probably make matters worse. So, now you know how I feel. I guess the question we need to think about now is, 'What would you like to do, and how can I help?'"

The principle of Mental Attending also implies self-awareness. In the section on Nonverbal Attending, you became aware that many of us fail to pay attention to how we come across to our partner. For instance, we may look in the mirror and not notice how we've let our physical appearance slide, yet our partner may be acutely aware of it and may even interpret it as a message that our affection and respect for our partner is "sliding" as well.

Our tendency to be unaware may come from three different perspectives. It could be that we simply were not taught how to be aware in our previous "life lessons." Or, maybe we were taught to be aware but, along the way, we became lazy regarding this lesson, and without practice, our ability to be aware diminished. Or it could be that we have a lot of things competing for our awareness, or attention, and we are too overwhelmed to attend to any one thing well. Unfortunately, the more complicated our lives become, the more our ability to be aware will be challenged. Consequently, mentally attending requires the ability to prioritize what we focus our time, senses, and energy on in order to efficiently manage the things competing for our attention.

The two mental attending skills we will address in this book are Visual Awareness and Listening Awareness. Each of these skills contains four sub-skills.

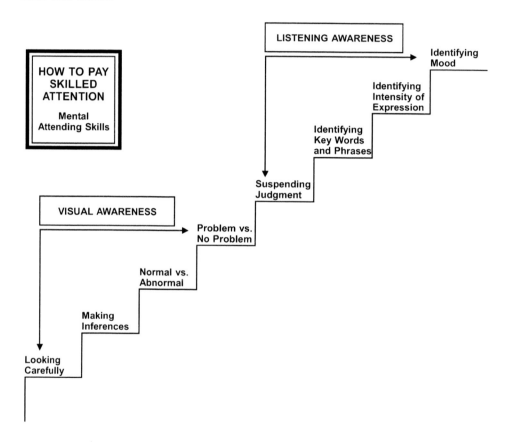

Visual Awareness

Visual Awareness is the ability to pay attention and understand your partner's appearances, behavior, and environment. Your careful obser-vation of actions, or behaviors, will tell you most of what you need to know about your partner including their feelings and their difficulties. The four steps in Visual Awareness are Looking Carefully, Making Infer-ences, deciding Normal vs. Abnormal, and deciding Problem vs. No Problem.

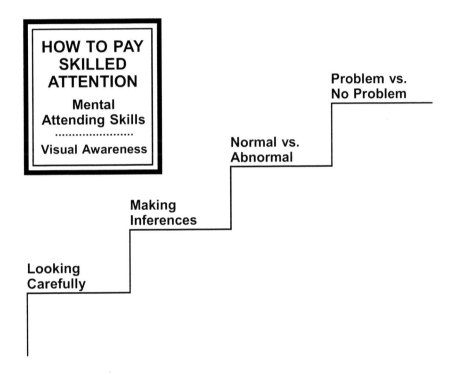

Looking Carefully

Looking carefully involves using your visual sense to observe another person's appearance, behavior, and environment.

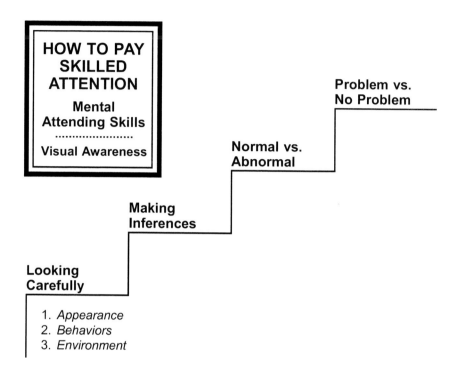

Looking Carefully: Appearance

Appearance refers to the nonverbal cues that a person might display even if he or she is unconscious or dead. For example, you might observe the following appearances: one person is African-American, one person didn't wear clean clothes today, one person is an older person, and one person is wearing a t-shirt and shorts.

Looking Carefully: Behavior

A **behavior** is a nonverbal cue that we usually observe in the form of *actions* that a person does while conscious and active. For example, you might observe any or all of the following behaviors: two people holding hands, one person hugging another, a person looking in a store window, a person wringing his or her hands.

How to Be in a Personal Relationship

Looking Carefully: Environment

Environment includes the physical settings people live, work, and play in (e.g., neighborhoods, homes, and the workplace) as well as the people they live with and relate to (e.g., friends, family, and co-workers). It also includes environmental experiences that have influenced their lives such as education, military service, vocation, and culture.

LOOKING CAREFULLY means observing another person's appearance, behavior, and environment.

When observing a person, you should ask yourself questions such as the following:

- "What are the important things about how he looks?" (*appearance*)

- "What's she doing right now?" (*behavior*)

- "What's important about where they are and who they're with?" (*environment*)

Once you're able to answer these questions, you're ready to draw some inferences about a person. For example, your partner has been going to work late (behavior), his clothes are wrinkled and his hair is unkempt (appearance), and recently he was turned down for a promotion at work (environment). The next step is to make inferences about what this information may mean.

DVD

LOOKING CAREFULLY: Appearance, Behavior, Environment
—The *Wrong* Way and the *Right* Way

Selena and Gabriel have been living together for about a year. Selena's mother found out about them living together, and she was not very happy. She has very strong religious convictions and believes that a man and a woman should be married if they are going to be living together. Consequently, she has not spoken to Selena in about six months.

Selena has always been very close to her mother, and she believes that she has let her mother down. The lack of communication between the two of them has greatly affected her. When Selena tries to talk to Gabriel about the situation and explain her feelings, he simply responds that her mom will eventually get over it and dismisses the conversation.

Tonight, Selena and Gabriel are having dinner when Selena mentions that she misses talking to her mother—after all, they used to talk two or three times a week. Gabriel reacts angrily by saying, "I'm sick and tired of hearing about this. As a matter of fact, I'm sick and tired of a lot of things. Ever since this thing happened with your mother, you've been a different person. We've just about stopped having sex lately. You go to bed *way* before me every night. You're gaining weight. And you don't seem to care about how you look any more. What's your problem!?"

Darlene and Darrell have been living together for two years. Recently Darlene has noticed that Darrell has not been acting like himself. When he comes home and first sees her, he says hello but doesn't walk up and kiss her. About two weeks ago, Darrell stopped coming to bed at night when Darlene would go to bed. In the past, he would sit with her and watch television in the bedroom while she read. Now, he goes into the other room and watches television.

Darlene has also noticed that Darrell hasn't been shaving and showering before going to bed. His hair is unkempt, and he only washes his hair every three days—a big change from what was fast becoming "the old Darrell." The other day, she noticed that he went to work wearing a work shirt that he had worn the day before (unlike him). The Darrell Darlene had loved and lived with for nearly two years had always been concerned about his appearance.

(continued)

As Darlene tried to figure out what was going on with Darrell, she reflected back on some of the other changes that had occurred in Darrell's life recently. His mom died about three months ago, and just the other night, Darrell and his dad had gotten into a heated argument over the phone. Darrell's dad remarried two weeks ago. When she considered all of this, Darrell's behaviors seemed a little more understandable to Darlene.

Making Inferences

Inferences are the initial assumptions you make as the result of observing people. You take in visual cues related to a person's appearance, behavior, and environment. These cues are really *clues* that show you something about a person's feelings, relationships, energy levels, and values. The more observations you make, the more inferences you can draw, and the more accurate these inferences will be. The four subskills in this section include how to make inferences about Feelings, Relationships, Energy Levels, and Values.

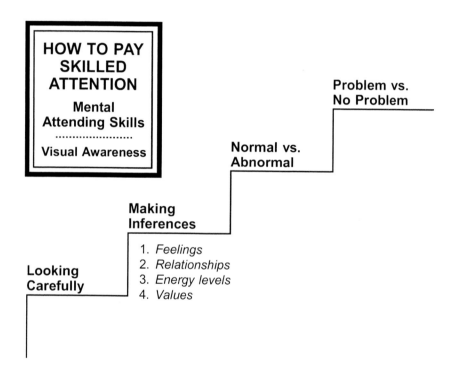

Inferences are important because they provide valuable information that increases your ability to help another person or predict that person's future behavior. Referring back to the previous "Making the Point," Darrell may be feeling sad and conflicted (feelings) due to the loss of his mother and his now strained relationship with his dad as he questions his dad's loyalty to his mother (value as son).

> **MAKING INFERENCES** means using your
> observations to determine a person's feelings,
> relationships, energy levels, and values.

Making Inferences: Feelings

You can use your looking carefully skills to draw inferences about how your partner is feeling. Knowing how your partner is feeling is critical in determining where he or she really is emotionally. For example, you might use the feeling word *happy* to describe a partner who is exercising and smiling. If you observe your partner pacing while wringing his/her hands, you might apply the feeling word *tense*. *Sad* might be used to describe a partner who seems to just sit and watch television.

> **MAKING INFERENCES ABOUT FEELINGS** means
> using your observations of a person's appearance,
> behaviors, and environment to determine
> what emotions the person is feeling.

Practice

What feeling word would you apply to the following examples?

1. A partner is sitting at his/her desk, head hanging down, clenching his/her fists, and staring straight ahead.

    Feeling word:_____

2. Sitting at the kitchen table, your partner is holding up a photograph while pointing to it and smiling broadly, laughing, and occasionally waving the photograph around.

    Feeling word:_____

Making the Point—The WRONG Way
The Case of the Insensitive Slob

Mai and Duc have been dating for a few months. Mai is having doubts about the relationship because of Duc's apparent insensitivity. Duc seems to be more concerned about himself than others.

Tonight, Duc has come to Mai's apartment, and they are about to go out for dinner. As they are about to leave, Mai receives a call from her mother. Her younger sister, Lin, has been in and out of trouble for years, and is a source of problems for her mother and the rest of the family—especially since their father died about five years ago. It has not been easy for Mai's mother trying to raise a teenage girl who has been acting out. Tonight, Lin has been arrested for drug possession, and Mai's mother doesn't know what to do. Mai looks over at Duc and tells him what is going on. Her voice is shaky, and she wears a very anxious look on her face.

Duc looks at Mai with an expression of disbelief and says, "You mean we aren't going to dinner? I've been looking forward to this all day long. You need to leave the little brat in jail and teach her a lesson."

Making the Point—The RIGHT Way
The Case of the Far-Sighted Woman

Maria and Enrique have been married for several years. They have no children. Maria found out years ago that she would not be able to conceive a child. Enrique loves children but has never brought up the subject of adoption to Maria. He believes that Maria would reject the idea because she never talks about children.

Last Sunday afternoon, they joined Enrique's family for dinner at his mother's home. Enrique has several nephews and nieces, and they all love Uncle Enrique! And it's obvious that Enrique really enjoys being around them as he plays with and attends to each one, from the biggest to the smallest.

That night, before going to bed, Maria asks Enrique to sit and talk to her. She starts the conversation by saying, "Today was so much fun. I couldn't help but notice that when you are around your nephews and nieces, you have the happiest look on your face. And whenever we leave after a day like today, I can't help but notice how sad and quiet you seem to get. I was wondering what you might think about the possibility of adopting a child of our own. What do you think?"

Enrique's eyes lit up like the sunrise. He was speechless at first. Then, he said, "Are you sure? Maria, I know how much you wanted to have children of your own. Are you sure about this?"

Marie had never been more sure of anything in her life.

How to Be in a Personal Relationship

Making Inferences: Relationships

Besides being aware of the behavior and appearance cues that indicate the feelings of a person, you can further increase your effectiveness by looking for cues that indicate the nature of the relationship between you and your partner. The relationship between you and your partner serves as a good indicator of future behavior between the two of you. If you have a good relationship with your partner, he or she may meet your needs without difficulty or conflict. If you have a poor relationship with your partner, he or she may not want to meet your needs, and the result could be conflict.

In general, you can categorize relationships and feelings as positive, negative, or neutral. Partners who do things to make your life easier (e.g., keep you informed) probably have, or want to have, a positive relationship with you. Partners who always try to hassle you (e.g., use abusive language, avoid you) either do not have or do not want to have a positive relationship with you. When a relationship is neutral, it is purely business with minimal emotional commitment—neither positive nor negative. In other words, the feelings are no longer there.

> **MAKING INFERENCES ABOUT RELATIONSHIPS**
> means using your observations of a person's
> appearance, behaviors, and environment
> to determine whether the relationship is
> positive, negative, or neutral.

Practice

List two behaviors and/or appearances that would tell you that your partner has a negative relationship with you.

Example: Goes to bed early and doesn't speak unless spoken to.

1. _____

_____

2. _____

_____

List two behaviors and/or appearances that would tell you that your partner has a positive relationship with you.

Example: Sits with you and will watch the TV programs you like.

1. _____

_____

2. _____

_____

Making the Point—The WRONG Way
The Case of the Missing Emotions

Rhonda and Sean have been married for about six years. They have no children, and they are both very involved in their jobs. Sean is a lawyer, and Rhonda is a business consultant. During the early years of their marriage, Rhonda told Sean that she did not want children until she was successful in her career.

Recently, Rhonda has been working long hours and going into the office on weekends. When Sean asks her to go to a movie or dinner, she responds that she's tired. Even though these rejections have been occurring regularly for the past three months, Sean has assumed that Rhonda is just going through something. After all, she has gone through periods of time in the past when she was difficult to get along with, and she has always gotten over it.

But this time, things seem different. Something is different about Rhonda's behavior these past six months—different from those other times. In the past, Rhonda would fly off the handle with Sean. She would get angry and be very critical of him. But then she would get over it and be nice to him for a few months. This time, Rhonda is showing no emotion. It's as if she has no feelings at all.

The next week, Rhonda tells Sean, "I've been thinking, and I'd like to focus on my career. It's the only thing that makes me happy."

How to Be in a Personal Relationship

Lucinda and Paul have been dating for four years. Lucinda has conveyed that she would like to get married in the next year. Paul says that he's not ready for that kind of a commitment yet.

Recently, Lucinda has become tired of Paul's procrastination. She has begun having lunch with a male co-worker because he is nice and pays attention to her. After a while, she feels guilty about these luncheons and decides she needs to be honest with Paul and tell him about the lunches and her feelings.

She calls Paul at work and tells him they need to talk. Paul meets her for dinner that night, and Lucinda says, "I love you, Paul, but I'm becoming ambivalent about our future. I'm starting to not like the way I'm feeling about our relationship. There's just no spark any more. I also don't like the way I'm acting." She goes on to explain the situation with the co-worker's attraction to her, and then she says, "I want to put our relationship back on a positive track. How about you?"

Although Paul is hurt and surprised, he keeps his cool and says, "Yes. I love you, and I want to fix things. Where do you think we go from here?"

Making Inferences: Energy Levels

Energy levels tell us a great deal about how a person will act. Energy is the capacity to act and maintain that act over time. For example, people with a low energy level are reluctant to initiate anything. They look and act defeated. Their movements are slow, their heads hang down, and every move seems like an effort. People with moderate energy levels actively engage in most activities (e.g., playing, working, talking, eating). High energy people not only participate in all that is required, but they may cause problems if they do not have constructive outlets for their energy. They tend to become bored easily, and they can be overbearing with those around them.

In a personal relationship, energy levels can become a source of conflict if there are incompatible energy levels between partners. *Changes* in energy levels are even more critical. People's energy levels are usually constant except at special times (e.g., weekends, special sporting events, and holidays). Abrupt changes from high to low to high energy levels may indicate a problem.

Practice

List two behaviors and/or appearances that show a high energy level.

Examples: Talking rapidly; dressing in a way that enhances the person's body shape and personality

1. _____

   _____

2. _____

   _____

List two behaviors and/or appearances that show a low energy level.

Examples: Watching a lot of TV; having a noticeable and unpleasant body odor

1. _____

   _____

2. _____

   _____

List two reasons that might cause energy levels to change.

Examples: Stress; the onset of a medical problem

1. _____

   _____

2. _____

   _____

Making the Point—The WRONG Way
The Case of Disconnected Desiree

Desiree and Zach have been married for two years. Normally, Zach is a very talkative person. From the time he gets up in the morning, he is ready to get the day under way. He immediately jumps into the shower, gets dressed, eats breakfast, and begins his daily activities.

Recently, he has told Desiree that there are a lot of layoffs at work, and he is concerned he could lose his job because he doesn't have much seniority. Today, Zach finally gets the word that he is going to be laid off. He decides he needs to tell Desiree when he first gets home rather than telling her over the phone.

When he walks in the door from work, he is obviously down. He has no energy. He tells Desiree about the layoff to which she responds, "When life gets tough, the tough get going." Zach counters her seeming harsh comment with, "Look, I love this job." Desiree does not hear the depth of his concern and hurt, and instead says, "You need to move on. By the way, are you going to finish painting the spare bedroom tonight? Remember, we've got company coming this weekend."

Zach looks at Desiree in disbelief, grabs his car keys, and leaves the house.

Making the Point—The RIGHT Way
The Case of Consuela's Concern

Consuela and Julio have been married for four years. They have no children. Julio is a high energy person who is constantly doing things. He can't sit still and gets bored quickly. On the other hand, Consuela has a moderate energy level. She is very task-oriented. She likes schedules and likes to sit and read.

Consuela and Julio have often had arguments about their incompatible energy levels. Julio thinks Consuela is not energetic enough and gets upset with her when she doesn't want to do all the things he does. Consuela counters by telling Julio that being around him is stressful.

Recently, Julio has been acting differently. He has been going to bed earlier than normal for him and sleeps later in the morning. His appearance is also changing. Normally, he gets up, even on his days off, and jumps into the shower, then changes into his clothes for the days' activities. Now he stays in his bed clothes until midmorning on the weekends.

Consuela decides to talk with Julio about this change in his appearance and behavior. To her dismay, she finds out that Julio has lost his job, and he has been avoiding telling her. For the past two weeks, he's been pretending that he has been going to work.

Making Inferences: Values

Every person has three basic environments: the place where he or she lives, the place where he or she works, and the place where he or she learns. In each of these settings, the actual "environment" will include not only physical materials but people—the people a person "hangs with." You can learn a great deal about people by carefully observing their environment. A general rule of thumb is that people give their energy to the things and people that are of value to them—the more energy given, the higher the value.

Values are the ideas (e.g., religious beliefs), things (e.g., automobiles, jewelry), and people (e.g., spouse, children) that a person has a strong bond with. Knowing what a person values has real implications for relating to them. When you know what a person wants and doesn't want, you've got an edge in maintaining a positive relationship.

> **MAKING INFERENCES ABOUT VALUES** means
> using your observations of a person's appearance,
> behaviors, and environment to determine
> what the person's values are.

Practice

List two of *your* important values:

1. _____

_____

2. _____

_____

List two of your *partner's* important values:

1. _____

_____

2. _____

_____

Making the Point—The WRONG Way
The Case of the Lame Excuse

Selena and Rick have been dating for several months. Recently, they got into a dispute over Selena wanting Rick to meet two old friends of hers. Selena had not seen these two friends in a couple of years, so she had arranged a dinner for them at her apartment. She really wanted Rick to meet them. Two weeks before the dinner was to take place, she and Rick talked about the dinner, and Rick promised he would be there.

On the night of the dinner, Selena's two friends arrived at her apartment right on time. Dinner was supposed to begin at 7:00 p.m. At 7:30 p.m., Rick had not shown up. Selena called Rick's cell phone and got his voicemail. At 8:00 p.m., Selena decided to start dinner without him. Around 9:30 p.m., Rick called saying he got her message, and he was sorry, but he had gotten interested in a football game on TV and totally forgot. When Selena heard what he had to say, she became upset and hung up the phone.

Rick did not call back for a week, and when he did, Selena said she didn't want to see him anymore.

Making the Point—The RIGHT Way
The Case of Observant Orlando

Rachel and Orlando have been dating for six months. While they have been dating, Orlando has noticed that Rachel never talks about her parents, but she often talks about her sister, Janna.

One day, Orlando decides to ask Rachel about her parents, but he quickly realizes that she becomes quiet and uncomfortable—looking away. He decides not to pursue asking about her parents, but instead, asks about her sister, Janna. At the mere mention of Janna's name, Rachel's face lights up, and she excitedly chatters about her sister and how much she cares about her. Orlando, sensing her excitement, says, "It's obvious to me how much you care for (value) your sister, Janna. I would really like to meet her. What if I take a couple of days off from work over the next couple of weeks, and we can go visit her?"

Rachel's eyes light up. Beaming, with a look that conveys how incredible and touched she feels by Orlando's suggestion, she looks him directly in the eyes and says, "You mean it!? That would be fantastic! I'll call her. You're gonna love her! And I know she's gonna love you, too!!"

Now, whenever you are making inferences, **the reasons for your inferences should be observable and concrete.** They should be *cues taken in by your senses* related to *behaviors, appearances,* and *environment.* Inferences stand the best chance of being accurate if they are **based on detailed and concrete observations** rather than on vague and general ones.

DVD

MAKING INFERENCES: Feelings, Relationships, Energy Levels, Values

—The *Wrong* Way and the *Right* Way

Practice

Read the following incident carefully. Be ready to give reasons (i.e., descriptions of appearances, behaviors, and environments) for some inferences you will be asked to draw.

> You are having dinner with a couple, Ben and Sandy, whom you have known for several years. When you first arrive at their home, you are met by Ben at the door. You overhear Sandy yelling in an angry tone from the bedroom, "I told you it wasn't a good idea—why did you do it?" You look at Ben's face as he rolls his eyes and says to you, "I'm glad you made it." Ben is a police officer, and you notice that he still has on his work uniform. As you enter the house, Ben says, "Why don't you go into the den and turn on the TV." He then turns and walks toward the bedroom where Sandy is. This seems strange. Normally when you go to Ben and Sandy's for dinner, Ben would ask you if you would like something to drink.
>
> Eventually, Sandy and Ben enter the den where you are sitting. Sandy doesn't acknowledge you but says, "I'll get dinner started." Ben then turns to you and says, "I'm sorry, but dinner's running a little late."
>
> In your past experiences with Sandy and Ben, Sandy has been someone who believes is social etiquette. It is unlike her *not* to say hello or *not* to have dinner ready. Ben has also been the type of person who wants to be the best host he can be.
>
> Now, you notice that Ben is still in his uniform, and his shirt has a food stain on it. It looks like he hasn't combed or washed his hair in a while. As he sits down next to you, he says in an uncharacteristic monotone voice, "How have you been? I'm glad you came by."

Making Inferences About Ben

Using the scenario above and the concepts you've learned in this section, complete the following questions. Then compare your answers to our answers on page 90.

Relationships

How is Ben relating to you? (positive, negative, neutral)

_____

Reason:

_____

_____

_____

_____

Feelings

What is Ben feeling? (angry, anxious, happy, confused, weak, etc.)

_____

Reason:

_____

_____

_____

_____

Energy Levels

What is Ben's energy level? (high, moderate, low)

_____

Reason:

_____

_____

_____

_____

(continued)

(concluded)

Values

What does Ben normally value? (people, ideas, things)

_____

Reason:

_____

_____

_____

_____

_____

Normal vs. Abnormal

Once you know someone, you begin to learn how they tend to function through your skills of visual awareness. One person is easy-going and hardly ever hassles you or anyone else. A second person always looks like he or she is mad at the world. A third always seems to be feeling sorry for him- or herself. Your ability to look carefully at others and the inferences you've drawn can help you determine whether a particular person is in a "Normal" or "Abnormal" condition for him- or herself at any point in time.

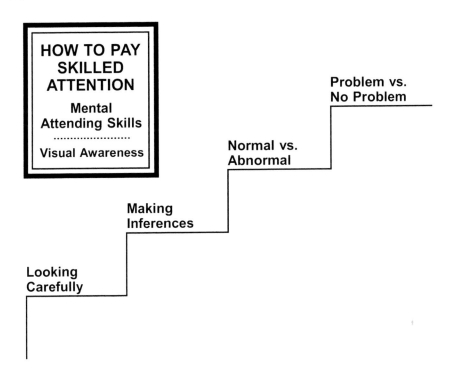

In determining whether things are normal or abnormal for a given person at a given time, compare your present observations with past ones. For example, you may observe a person talking loudly with another person. If this is normal behavior for this person, you probably need to exercise only the usual amount of caution. But if the appearance and behavior of the angry person are highly unusual or abnormal for them, you'll know it's a potentially troublesome situation.

> **VISUAL AWARENESS** means determining
> if a person's actions and/or situation are normal
> or abnormal based on your observations and any
> prior knowledge you have of that person.

For example, normal behavior for Ben, mentioned previously in the practice exercise, is to smile when he initially sees you and be very animated in his voice tone. His normal appearance is to keep his hair neatly combed and washed regularly, and to have his clothes pressed and creased perfectly, with shoes polished. He normally offers you a drink. On this particular night, however, his behavior and appearance have changed. He is not smiling very much, not animated, his clothes and shoes are stained and dull, and he directs you to the den without offering you a drink.

DVD

NORMAL vs. ABNORMAL
— The *Wrong* Way and the *Right* Way

Practice

In the previous scenario involving Ben, is Ben's situation and/or actions normal or abnormal? Yes or no?

Give Reason:

_____

_____

_____

_____

_____

How to Be in a Personal Relationship

Making the Point—The WRONG Way
The Case of Too Little, Too Late

Jacque is a successful high school football coach. He has been coaching for over 30 years. His wife, Kayla, has been very patient about Jacque's love of coaching and all the time it has taken from their relationship. Throughout their life together, she has focused her attention on raising their four children, trying to fill the void created by Jacque's many absences.

This past year, their last child, Rosemary, moved away from home to attend college, and there are now no children at home for Kayla to care for. Their two older children now live in other states, and their third child is in the military.

Jacque decides to call Kayla after football practice to say he is running late. He is going to review some of the game films. It's after 7:00 in the evening, and he's a little surprised Kayla isn't home. She doesn't like to be out after dark because she doesn't like to drive at night—the glare of oncoming headlights hurts her eyes. He rationalizes that she must be having a good time out shopping and settles in to watch the films.

Jacque decides to head home around 9:00 p.m. As he enters the house, there are no lights on. It is eerily quiet. It doesn't feel normal. He calls out Kayla's name. There is no answer. He enters the bedroom and flips the light switch on. Kayla is lying on the bed—too still, listless. He notices a bottle of pills on the night stand, and he rushes to her side. Unable to rouse her, he calls 911, but it's too late. His Kayla has died, and she has not left any notes or evidence to tell him or the children why.

In the midst of his grief, Jacque begins to reflect on Kayla's apparent suicide. He wondered why he never saw it coming. Memories begin to flood his mind. She had mentioned she was having trouble sleeping (not normal for her). He also noticed that she seemed less talkative lately (not the norm for her). Come to think of it, she had repeatedly mentioned that she needed to spend more time with him—something she rarely expressed in years past. Then he looked around him, and for the first time, he realized that Kayla had not kept up the house the way she normally had. Kayla had always enjoyed being kidded about being a "neat freak." The kids were always complaining about it. Somehow, he hadn't noticed that she had stopped being a "neat freak" for the past several months.

Jacque was heart broken. All the signs had been there. He should have seen it coming. He couldn't believe that his Kayla was gone. He was grief stricken, and he felt selfish. He had been so wrapped up in his own world, he had completely let Kayla down. She had always supported him, never complaining, and when she reached out for him, he hadn't been there. Being there now was too little, too late.

Problem vs. No Problem

As with your decision regarding Normal vs. Abnormal, the decision you make regarding whether a person may present Trouble or No Trouble should be based on your observations and your knowledge of that person. When we talk about a "problem" in this section, we are referring to the observations of any abrupt and/or major changes in a person's behavior and/or appearance that could mean trouble.

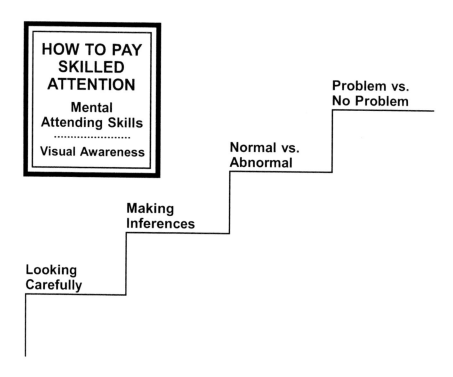

VISUAL AWARENESS means determining whether a person might present a problem or no problem based on your observations and any prior knowledge you have of that person.

 DVD

PROBLEM vs. NO PROBLEM
— The *Wrong* Way and the *Right* Way

Practice

In the previous scenario involving Ben, is Ben likely experiencing a problem or no problem? Yes or no?

Give Reason:

_____

_____

_____

_____

_____

Making the Point—The RIGHT Way
The Case of Oscar's Observation

Jasmine and Oscar have been married for eight years. They have dual careers and two small children who are at daycare during the day. The fact that Jasmine has a great job making an exceptional salary allows Oscar to have a lot of "big boy" toys (e.g., a nice car, two houses, a golf membership, etc.).

Recently, Jasmine has been acting withdrawn from Oscar. She doesn't seem to be interested in sex. She doesn't mention her job, and she doesn't ask him about his job. The only thing she seems to enjoy is being with the children when she gets home from work. Recently, although Oscar thought they had discussed the issue thoroughly and were in agreement, Jasmine has mentioned that she may want to put off selling their current home in order to move to a more expensive home in an upscale neighborhood.

Oscar decides that there is a problem, and it needs to be addressed. He calls his mother and asks her to pick up the kids at daycare. He is going to meet Jasmine after work.

After Oscar picks up Jasmine at work, he drives to a local park. He then tells Jasmine what he has observed in her behaviors lately. He has come to the conclusion that her behaviors are not normal, and there is a problem.

Reluctantly, she says there is a problem. She tells him she wants to be a "stay at home" mom. She doesn't care about the money anymore. She misses her children. She doesn't want a fancy house.

After listening to all that Jasmine has to say, Oscar says, "I love you, and I'll do whatever it takes to get you happy again."

Answers to Practice on pp. 83–84

Relationships

How is Ben relating to you? (Positive, Negative, Neutral)

Neutral

Reason:

When he sits down, his tone of voice is flat and unemotional.

Feelings

What is Ben feeling? (angry, anxious, happy, confused, weak, etc.)

anxious

Reason:

He is trying to attend to your arrival while Sandy, who appears to be angry with him, is in the other room.

Energy Levels

What is Ben's energy level? (high, moderate, low)

low

Reason:

He is still in his uniform when you arrive, he is in conflict with Sandy, and he is having to pay attention to you.

Values

What does Ben normally value? (people, ideas, things)

His relationships

Reason:

Normally, he is very attentive when you arrive at his house by

offering you something to drink and by being dressed for the

occasion (i.e., not in his work clothes).

Action Strategies

Below are some Visual Awareness Strategies you may want to use in your personal relationships if the situation allows for it.

1. List five behaviors that your partner typically exhibits during the day.
   Example: Shave every morning before showering, or read every evening when first going to bed.

   a. _____

   _____

   b. _____

   _____

   c. _____

   _____

   d. _____

   _____

   e. _____

   _____

2. List three typical appearances that your partner typically exhibits most days.

   Example: Wears sweat pants on weekends most of the day, or hair is always combed.

   a. _____

   _____

   b. _____

   _____

   c. _____

   _____

3. Look at your partner's behavior and appearance, and infer how they might be feeling.

   Walk up and say, "You look _____ (fill in the blank with the emotion—happy, sad, anxious, etc.)."

   _____

   _____

   _____

   _____

   _____

4. Think of three occasions when you were relating to your partner. Record whether the interaction was positive, negative, or neutral. Then, write down the behaviors they exhibited that made you give that rating as well as what was going on in **their** environment at the time.

   a. _____

   _____

   b. _____

   _____

   c. _____

   _____

5. Think of three occasions when you were relating to your partner. Record whether their energy level appeared high, moderate, or low. Then write down the behaviors and appearances they exhibited that made you give that rating as well as what was going on in **their** environment at the time.

a. _____

_____

b. _____

_____

c. _____

_____

Now, write a Visual Awareness Action Strategy:

_____

_____

_____

_____

_____

Skills Summary
Visual Awareness

Now let's review all of the skills and sub-skills involved in Visual Awareness.

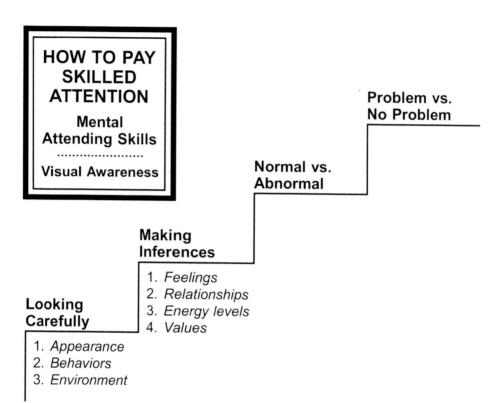

Listening Awareness

Listening is the ability to hear and understand what your partner is really saying. Listening helps you hear not only the words your partner is saying but the emotions behind them.

The four steps in listening awareness are Suspending Judgment, Identifying Key Words and Phrases, Identifying Intensity of Expression, and Identifying Mood.

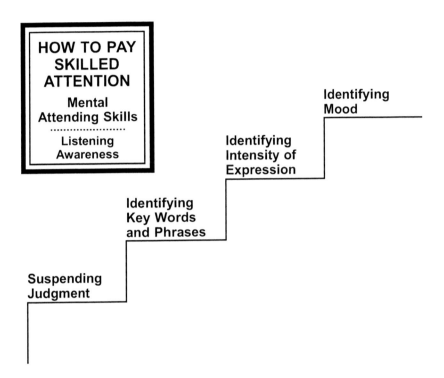

A good listener can often prevent problems because people often go through "verbal stages" before the action begins. If you can hear the signals, you may be able to head off any trouble before it really begins. Listening involves your ability to hear and accurately recall all of the *important* verbal cues used by people. *Important* verbal cues are those that may imply signs of trouble or problems.

In our personal relationships, complaints are common, of course, but they're also important. An effective partner listens to complaints and recognizes when a familiar cue is uttered in a new tone or when a complaint arises from a normally uncomplaining partner. An effective partner listens especially for changes: silence when there is usually noise or noise when there is usually silence. Once again, the partner asks him- or herself the question, "Is there a problem here? Am I missing something?"

Getting ready to listen. You should get ready for listening by using the nonverbal attending skills and visual awareness skills whenever possible.

- **Arranging:** Arranging your environment to eliminate distractions and to make it pleasant will help you focus on your partner when he/she is talking.

- **Positioning:** Properly positioning yourself will obviously help you to better hear what the speaker has to say.

- **Posturing:** Posturing is essential when you're listening to a person who really wants to talk to you. Your posture can signal to the person that you're focusing all your attention on him or her.

- **Gesturing:** Gesturing aids your listening because the gesturing behaviors you display can either distract from or motivate the speaker to keep talking.

- **Facing:** Good eye contact and appropriate facial expressions facilitate listening. The speaker often looks at the listener's face to determine the listener's willingness to listen.

- **Vocalizing:** The tone of voice given off by the listener is an indicator to the speaker as to the emotional state of the listener.

- **Appearing:** The way you look, from a grooming standpoint, may indicate to the speaker your level of alertness. If you appear unkempt, the speaker may think you are too tired to listen.

- **Touching:** Sometimes, touching a person while they are speaking makes them want to talk more.

- **Looking Carefully:** Your observing skills can always be used to promote better listening. For example, you may overhear something that someone is talking about in another room. But your *visual observations* help you understand the implications of what you're hearing. Someone who sounds angry but is leaning back in a chair and grinning may only be telling an entertaining story, while someone whose angry voice "fits" with a tense, uptight appearance may present a very different situation.

- **Making Inferences:** Remember that careful observations about a person's appearance, behaviors, and environment will help you make accurate inferences about that person's feelings, relationships, energy levels, and values.

- **Normal vs. Abnormal:** Decide whether a person's current condition is normal or abnormal based on your current *and past* observations.

- **Problem vs. No Problem:** Using both your previous and your current observations of the person, determine whether this person is now displaying any abrupt changes in his or her appearance or behaviors that could indicate trouble.

There is one more preliminary thing: you can't listen effectively to your partner if you've got other things on your mind. If you're thinking about job responsibilities, you may miss a lot of what is said and what it really means. You've got to focus on your partner—and that takes a *lot* of concentration. You can work to develop this kind of concentration by reviewing what you're going to do and with whom you're going to do it before you begin. Then, you'll really be ready to start using the four specific procedures that skilled listening involves.

Suspending Judgment

Suspending judgment is very difficult for anyone to do, especially when emotions are involved. If, however, your goal is to get more information about a situation, you will need to get your partner to open up more. Suspending judgment, at least temporarily, can assist with that.

It is still hard at times to listen without immediately judging because your partner may get defensive (e.g., clam up, get upset, or become vague) very quickly when you try to talk with them. Despite this, it will severely hamper your efforts if you do not suspend judgment because you will never hear the real verbal cues you need in order to fully understand what's going on.

Suspending judgment requires you to control your nonverbal cues, your verbal cues, and your thoughts.

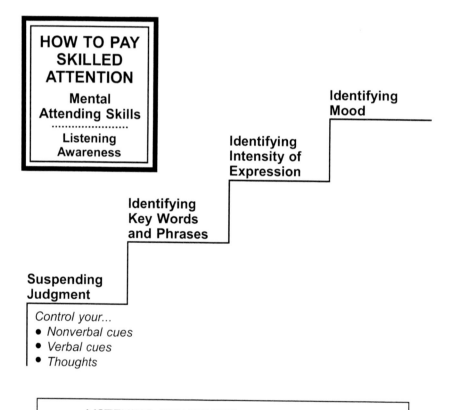

HOW TO PAY SKILLED ATTENTION
Mental Attending Skills
·····················
Listening Awareness

Identifying Mood

Identifying Intensity of Expression

Identifying Key Words and Phrases

Suspending Judgment
Control your...
• Nonverbal cues
• Verbal cues
• Thoughts

LISTENING AWARENESS means **suspending your judgment** temporarily so that you can really hear what is being said.

How to Be in a Personal Relationship

Suspending Judgment: Control Your Nonverbal Cues

The first lesson to learn in this section is how to avoid giving off any nonverbal behaviors that might indicate that you are judging. For example, your facial expressions, your gestures, and/or your tone of voice can be indicators to the speaker that you are uneasy or emotionally judging what they are saying. These types of signals can act to cut a conversation short or even change the content of what is being said.

Suspending Judgment: Control Your Verbal Cues

The second lesson to learn is how to control the words that come out of your mouth that might indicate that you are judging. If you use words in your responses to the person speaking that imply you are judging *either* the speaker or what the speaker is saying, he or she may "clam up" or simply resort to telling you what he or she *thinks* you want to hear.

Suspending Judgment: Control Your Thoughts

The third lesson is to keep your thoughts about what you're hearing nonjudgmental. Imagine for a moment that while a person is speaking to you, the little voice in your head is saying, "Yeah, right," or "I knew they were hiding something." More often than not, what you are really thinking will leak out in your body language or your words. The result is that the speaker senses that you are judging him or her, and again, the person will become quiet or share with you only what they think you want to hear or can handle, but not the full story.

DVD

SUSPENDING JUDGMENT
— The *Wrong* Way and the *Right* Way

Making the Point—The WRONG Way
The Case of the Suspicious Mind

Julianne and Rex have been having difficulties in their relationship for the past six months. Rex suspects that Julianne may be seeing someone else. Julianne is not seeing anyone else, but she is constantly being called at work by her ex-boyfriend. Julianne wants to tell Rex, but he has a temper, and this might make things worse.

One evening while Julianne and Rex are having dinner, Julianne decides that she needs to tell Rex about the ex-boyfriend's calls at work. As soon as she mentions the ex-boyfriend's name, Rex gives her a facial display of anger. Julianne decides not to talk about it any further. When she becomes quiet, Rex immediately says in an angry tone, "I knew you were seeing him. I knew I couldn't trust you."

Julianne immediately gets up and leaves the restaurant. Rex follows her outside and tries to apologize. Julianne then says, "You know, I like to be truthful, but you just can't handle it."

Making the Point—The RIGHT Way
The Case of Rex's Regret

Julianne and Rex have left the restaurant and are driving back to Julianne's apartment. Rex is feeling guilty about overreacting to Julianne's attempt to explain the harassing calls from her ex-boyfriend. Rex decides to keep quiet while Julianne starts to open up about the problem.

She begins by telling Rex that she tried to tell him about the ex-boyfriend's harassment several times but he either acted like he wasn't listening or he began to get angry with her when it wasn't her fault. As she continues, Julianne brings up things she tried to tell Rex about her ex. She says, "I remember telling you that my father and my ex-boyfriend's father are in business together, and you said, 'Yeah' and changed the subject. I remember telling you that my dad didn't understand why I broke it off with my ex, and I didn't tell him the truth because of my dad's relationship with his dad. You acted like you didn't hear me and started talking on your cell phone to a friend."

Identifying Key Words and Phrases

There are key words and phrases to listen for whenever you are listening to another person—and especially when you are listening to what your partner is saying. Here are a few key words and phrases that you might want to attend to: *bills, lonely, time, unsure, "need a break," "your fault."* When identifying key words and phrases, you must consider the person and the context.

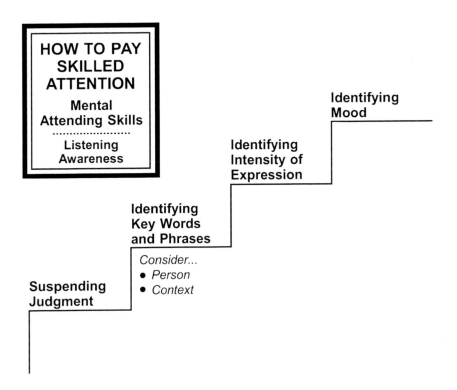

Of course, everything you hear must be considered in terms of who said it. After all, all of us probably know at least one person who always seems to be complaining about something (by the way, don't be fooled by this person—you still need to use your listening awareness skills when they are speaking to make sure you don't miss something important!). In addition to identifying the speaker, it's also important to identify the context in which the key words and phrases are spoken as well as the circumstances and characteristics of the relationship between the speaker and listener, and add to these your observations to determine what inferences, responses, and/or actions are appropriate for you to make.

> **LISTENING AWARENESS** means **identifying the key words and phrases,** such as *bills, sex, children,* and *need a break,* based on your knowledge of the person speaking and the context.

DVD

IDENTIFYING KEY WORDS AND PHRASES
— The *Wrong* Way and the *Right* Way

Practice

List some words and phrases that signal trouble in your particular relationship.

Example:

Word/Phrase	Circumstances
Bills	Money problems in relationship
Can't commit	Dating a long time
Unhappy	Partner constantly critical of you

You write three:

1. Word/Phrase: _____
   Circumstances: _____

2. Word/Phrase: _____
   Circumstances: _____

3. Word/Phrase: _____
   Circumstances: _____

How to Be in a Personal Relationship

Making the Point—The WRONG Way
The Case of Marty the Mind Reader

Jeannie and Marty have been dating for about a year. Recently, they got into a shouting match over the direction of their relationship. Jeannie believes he doesn't really pay attention to her actual words. To her, it seems he is always interpreting her statements. Below is an excerpt from their recent disagreement:

Jeannie: I wish you would quit putting my friends down. They are important to me.

Marty: So, you're saying you would rather be with your friends than with me.

Jeannie: No, that's not what I said. But when you keep taking my words and twisting them into something I didn't say, I don't like being around you.

Marty: That's right! Every time things don't go your way, you want to end the relationship.

Jeannie: See! This is what I'm talking about. I *don't* want to end the relationship. I just want you to listen to me and hear what I am actually saying—not what you *think* I'm saying.

Marty: Oh! So now you think I'm not smart enough to know what you really mean when you say something.

Jeannie: Ah! So, now you think you're a mind reader? You actually believe you know what I'm thinking? *That's your problem!* You really don't listen to what I am actually saying because you think there's a hidden meaning. Now I *do* need a break from you!

Making the Point—The RIGHT Way
The Case of Leon's Listening Skills

Deanna and Leon have been married for five years. They have a great relationship. Deanna has always said that one of the things she liked about Leon was his ability to listen. Below is an excerpt from a recent conversation they were having about their relationship:

Deanna: Lately, I've been feeling like we aren't spending enough time alone. We're either at work, with our friends, or with our parents. I'd like to do something alone with you.

Leon: You think we need to spend some time alone and not just with family and friends?

Deanna: Yeah! I mean, think about it. On Fridays, you go out with the guys from work and bowl. I go out with friends and see a movie. On Saturday nights, we are usually with Bob and Sally or Gary and Kathy. On Sundays, we usually go to your parents for dinner. It's not that I don't enjoy that, but once in a while, on weekends, I'd like for it to be just you and me.

Leon: So, let me make sure I understand what you're saying. You like what we do with family and friends on weekends, but you'd also like for us to be alone on a Friday, Saturday, or Sunday once in a while.

Deanna: Yes! That's it! I do love being with friends and family on weekends, but not all the time.

How to Be in a Personal Relationship

Identifying Intensity of Expression

Statements are made with varying levels of intensity (high, moderate, and low). *Intensity* is a key word here. *Intensity* comes from the word *intense*. The word *intense* implies how much tension is inside a person at that moment. Therefore words that have a lot of tension behind them (intensity of expression) are key words because of their connection to emotions within that person. When identifying the intensity of an expression, you must determine if the intensity level is high, moderate, or low.

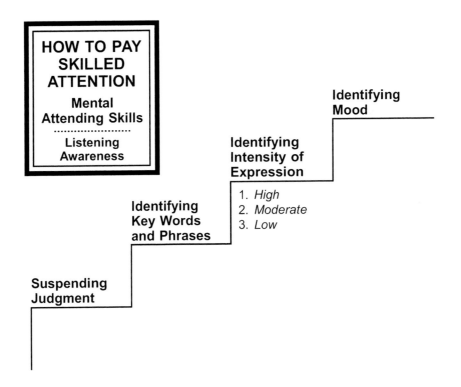

The louder and more emotional a statement, the more intense it is. But "loudness" and "emotion" *are not* the same thing. A wavering voice, for example, signals a lot of emotion, even though it may not be loud. A statement that is either loud or emotional, but not both, is most often of moderate intensity. A statement that is loud and empty of emotion is usually of low intensity. High intensity statements are very real signs of danger.

> **LISTENING AWARENESS** means determining
> whether the *intensity* of a person's speech is
> *high, moderate, or low.*

If your partner is talking with you, and you become aware of changes in your partner's voice intensity when he or she says certain words or phrases, these are cues for you to pay close attention to those words and/or phrases. For example, high intensity behind the following phrases can be important: "I've had it," "I'm out of here," "Don't do it again," "I mean it," "I really love you," "You're special to me," "I can't wait to see you."

DVD

IDENTIFYING INTENSITY OF EXPRESSION
— The *Wrong* Way and the *Right* Way

Making the Point—The WRONG Way
The Case of Sara the Staller

Sara and Bart have been dating for several months. They have even been talking about marriage, but Bart is still uneasy about Sara's level of commitment to a long-term relationship. He decides he wants to discuss it with her before he takes the next step and purchases an engagement ring.

They are walking in the park on a Saturday afternoon. Bart asks Sara to sit on one of the park benches. After they are seated, he starts out by saying he wants to talk about the relationship. Bart tells Sara that he is serious about the possibility of marriage.

Initially, Sara says she doesn't want to talk about it. Bart presses her. Sara then says, "I *do* want to get married" (her voice intensity is low, implying emotional doubt). She goes on to say, "Of course I do. How could you think otherwise?" (again, with low intensity of expression). Then, she yawns and says, "Let's keep walking in the park. I was really enjoying that" (spoken with a higher intensity of expression and a sense of aggravation in her voice tone).

Bart says, "I'm glad to hear that you really want to get married. I'm glad you are finally 100 percent sure this is what you want to do."

How to Be in a Personal Relationship

Making the Point—The RIGHT Way
The Case of Hesitant Hal

Juanita and Hal have been together for several years. Hal says that Juanita is one of those people you can't hide much from. She is very perceptive, which he finds refreshing because he has a problem expressing his true feelings.

Juanita asks Hal how he feels about the two of them visiting family in California. Hal replies (in a hesitant tone), "I'm fine with it. You do anything you like."

Juanita responds, "You're saying it's okay, but I hear hesitancy in your voice." Hal says (in an anxious tone of voice), "I want you to go, but I'm not sure I can get time off from work."

Juanita responds, "Okay. But I don't know if it's just the time off from work that's making you anxious. You sound anxious about making the trip at all."

Hal replies (anxiety in his voice), "Well, I really don't want you to go without me. Can we wait 'til I get my vacation time built up so that I can go?" Juanita responds, "Sure."

Identifying Mood

Moods are important to assess because they affect our thinking and, therefore, our words and actions. If the circumstances of a situation stay the same but the mood of the person in that situation changes, that same person may think, speak, and act differently despite the same circumstances. *Mood* here means, at a very simple level, what your partner is *feeling*. Moods may be positive, negative, or neutral, and it is critical that you can identify the mood as either normal or abnormal.

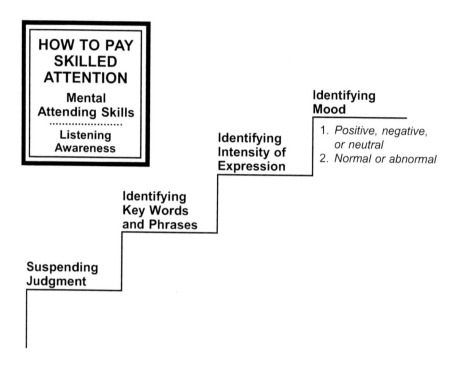

Identifying Mood: Positive, Negative, or Neutral

Is your partner's mood positive, negative or neutral? Why? One question you may ask to determine mood is, "What kinds of feelings are being expressed or implied (positive, negative, or neutral)?"

> **LISTENING AWARENESS** means identifying
> whether a mood is positive, neutral, or negative.

How to Be in a Personal Relationship

Identifying Mood: Normal or Abnormal

Another question you want to answer is, "Is this mood normal or abnormal for my partner under the circumstances?" Sure, there are always exceptions. For example, your partner can say, "I'm going to leave you," quietly and without emotion, yet still mean it. This is why it is so important to know as much as possible and continue to observe and listen for other cues.

> **LISTENING AWARENESS** means identifying
> whether a mood is normal or abnormal.

DVD

IDENTIFYING MOOD
— The *Wrong* Way and the *Right* Way

Making the Point—The WRONG Way
The Case of Bo the Befuddled

Tonya and Bo have been married for two years. They have been arguing frequently for the past two months. The problem is that Tonya doesn't like her job, but she doesn't want to tell Bo because they need the money—now more than ever. Bo recently bought an expensive motorcycle and a boat, against Tonya's wishes.

It is now Friday evening and they are out with friends. Tonya is tired because she has gone through another week at a job she can't stand. She would rather be home than out with friends. Bo is being his typical boisterous self.

Tonya finally says to Bo, "I would like to go home soon. It's almost ten o'clock." She says it in a polite, but fatigued, tone of voice. Bo looks at her and says (in an annoyed tone), "I'm having a good time, and you want to ruin it."

Tonya stands up from the table and says, "I'm tired, Bo, and I want to go home." Bo looks at her and says angrily, "What is your problem?"

Tonya storms off, saying she is going to the ladies' room. In reality, she goes to the front of the restaurant and requests a cab to take her home.

After about 30 minutes, Bo goes to look for Tonya. Finally one of the other friends tells him that Tonya took a cab home.

Sheila and Ray have been together for ten years. Sheila is one of those people who wears a perpetual smile when she is around others. Ray would describe Sheila as a very positive person, and he says that even when she's tired, she tries to project a positive attitude.

Recently, Sheila and Ray were at a party with several long-term friends. Ray noticed that Sheila was quiet as they drove to the party, which was not normal for her. Sheila has always liked parties with their friends, so it seemed out of character for her. When they reached the party, Sheila greeted everybody with an open smile, but something was missing. One of Sheila's friends commented to Ray that Sheila didn't seem like herself tonight.

When Sheila and Ray got home that night, Ray asked her what was wrong. Sheila said everything was fine, but Ray thought he knew better, and he pushed it again. Sheila became irritated and told him to let it go, so Ray backed off.

About an hour later, Sheila approached Ray. She apologized and then said, "Ray, I went to the doctor last week and had some tests. The doctor called today and told me I have early indications of cervical cancer."

Action Strategies

Below are some Listening Strategies you may want to use in your personal relationships if the situation allows for it:

1. Sit across from your partner and ask him/her how his/her day went. Suspend judgment by maintaining control of all your nonverbal attending behaviors. Do this on *three* occasions.

2. Sit across from your partner and ask him/her to tell you something he/she would like you to change about yourself or do differently. If they tell you, *do not think about anything else* while you are listening to the feedback, and *do not show any judgment* in your nonverbal attending.

3. Sit across from your partner when he/she is telling you something. After your partner finishes, identify the key words and phrases you recall him/her saying. Do this on *three* occasions.

4. On *three* occasions after your partner has spoken and finished, say the following: "So you're telling me _____" and try to *relate back to him/her what you heard until he/she accepts it as accurate.*

5. After your partner has conveyed something to you, write down the words or phrases you heard that had the most changes in intensity of expression (change of volume/tone).

_____
_____
_____
_____
_____

Now, write a Listening Awareness Action Strategy:

_____
_____
_____
_____
_____

Skills Summary
Listening Awareness

Now let's review all of the skills and sub-skills involved in Listening Awareness.

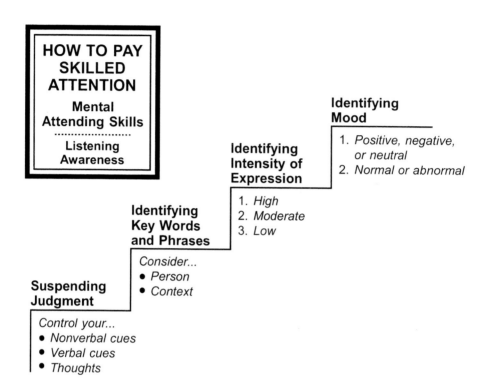

How to Be in a Personal Relationship

Skills Summary
Mental Attending Skills

Now let's review all of the skills and sub-skills involved in Mental Attending.

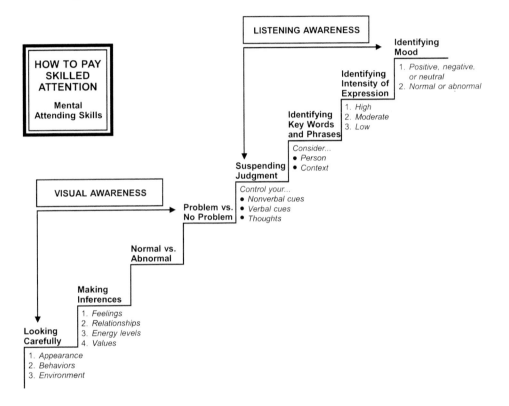

Section II

Emotion Management

Emotions can be defined as the feelings we experience in our bodies either due to our inherent nature or due to how we've been nurtured. In other words, nature may dictate the rise of some emotions (e.g., sexual desire for someone you've only seen from across a crowded room but as yet have not been introduced to), but many of our feelings are the result of our past experiences, what we've been taught by our family or friends, and/or the beliefs of our society and/or culture.

In your own life, think of times when you may have experienced emotions that felt out of your control. Maybe you were in an unfamiliar place, and you felt apprehensive—you didn't know why, but you sure felt it. That may have been your "nature" side trying to inform you about a threat you couldn't recognize.

Your "nurture" side is the result of your life experiences. For instance, think of a past experience that resulted in a persistent emotion. One of the authors remembers a scary encounter with a large dog as a child which led to feeling afraid of large dogs for many years afterward—even though none of those dogs had actually behaved threateningly. Or think of how you have been taught to feel by family or friends. Do you remember the old saying, "Blood is thicker than water," and how that implies emotional ties to family members? Were you ever put in a position in school where, as a member of a group, you may have developed feelings of distrust or dislike for people who weren't members of your group? And think of how our society or culture influences our emotions. Some societies or cultures foster feelings of hate for other societies or cultures. Many religious institutions within our societies preach "love thy neighbor." Our societies and cultures also tell us if it is appropriate to cry openly at a funeral or laugh loudly at a comedy.

Besides understanding where our feelings come from, it is important to realize that our emotions are felt and expressed with varying levels of intensity. Terms such as *sensitive, sentimental*, and *passionate* are terms used to describe people whose emotional makeup is intense. Terms such as insensitive, uncaring, detached, and cold are terms used to describe people who seem to have very little emotion or no emotion.

Regardless of where our emotions come from or how intense they are, it is essential that we recognize the power that our emotions can have. They can drive us to think thoughts that are not rational and lead us to act in ways that can harm ourselves or others. It's not unusual for us to experience a feeling that is completely inappropriate and unfounded. As a result, we begin to look for *any* information that will confirm our belief. If we are confronted with information that "proves" we are wrong, we tend to dismiss that information and continue looking for "data" to support our position—even if our quest for more information becomes destructive to us, to others, or to our relationship(s). To that end, one of the most valuable skills you can develop is how to manage the emotions of both yourself and others.

The management of our emotions is a critical component to a successful relationship, whether that relationship is intimate (i.e., with your partner) or platonic (i.e., at work, with your friends, or in the community). Yes, your "nature" may be behind the sudden feeling of sexual attraction to another person, but if you are already in a committed relationship, and your goal is to maintain that relationship, then you have to manage that feeling so that you can honor your current relationship. Likewise, the feeling of fear is a critical component that contributes to our ability to survive, but if a person doesn't learn how to manage his or her fear—especially when it's just a "feeling" and there is no evidence to suggest that a threat truly exists—that person may retreat away from social interactions and find themselves isolated and lonely. Even cultures struggle with the question of how to manage emotions. Some cultures believe that expressing emotions is an indication of weakness or a lack of control. Other cultures believe that the free expression of emotion is desirable because it indicates genuineness or realness.

For the sake of this training, it will be stressed that neither the complete control of emotion nor the free expression of emotion is the best way to manage one's emotions. Instead, we propose that the regulation, or managing, of emotions is the most effective route.

Regulating emotion is the ability to keep your destructive emotions under control. Further, if someone needs to express negative emotions, he or she must learn to manage the emotion internally in a way that is constructive (rather than destructive) and healthy. If those negative emotions are constructively dealt with internally, they will more likely be expressed in a constructive manner.

There are three major skills necessary for managing our emotions: Recognizing, Reasoning, and Relating.

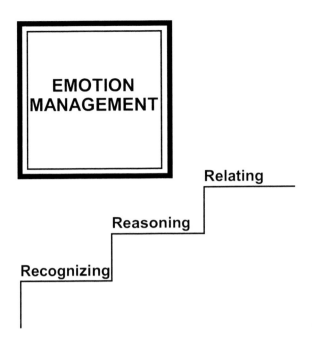

EMOTION
MANAGEMENT

Relating

Reasoning

Recognizing

Recognizing

Recognizing emotions is the ability to acknowledge the emotions we and others are experiencing at any given time. This helps us be aware of our emotions and the emotions of others. There are many instances where emotions that are acted upon without awareness can be destructive.

For example, you become very angry with a partner but ignore it. All of a sudden you say something to them that is sarcastic or hurtful due to your unacknowledged anger. Then they react with sarcasm and painful words toward you, and an argument ensues.

Or let's say you don't see or hear the fatigue in a loved one's face or voice when he/she comes home from work. You make a request of your partner that requires him/her to expend a lot of energy. Because your partner is fatigued, he/she becomes irritated with your request. You are surprised at the apparent abrupt anger at you, and so you become angry. Then the argument begins.

Recognizing emotions is an important skill because it can prevent emotional acting out or the escalation of negative emotions. Recognizing emotions is the first step in regulating your emotions.

There are three sub-skills in Recognizing Emotions: Categorizing, Measuring Intensity, and Naming.

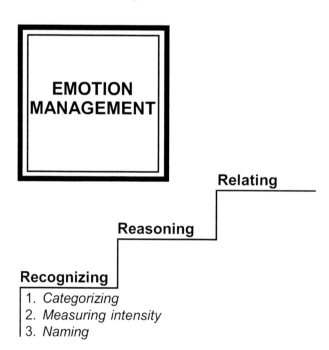

EMOTION MANAGEMENT

Relating

Reasoning

Recognizing
1. *Categorizing*
2. *Measuring intensity*
3. *Naming*

Recognizing: Categorizing

A method for recognizing yours and others' emotions is to determine which of the basic human emotions you or they are experiencing at a given time. There are seven basic emotional categories:

- Happy
- Angry
- Sad
- Confused
- Scared
- Strong
- Weak

Categorizing helps, because when our emotions begin to overwhelm us, we often lack the ability to be precise in identifying our emotions. Categorizing is the first step because it is the simplest step in identifying our emotions.

For example, if we are looking for a specific location on a map, it becomes much easier to find that location when we are in the vicinity of it. When you are able to select the correct category of emotions (e.g., happy), it gets you closer to the specific emotion you are looking for (e.g., pleased).

RECOGNIZING EMOTIONS means being
able to correctly *identify* the *category* of
emotion being expressed.

DVD

RECOGNIZING EMOTION: Categorizing
— The *Wrong* Way and the *Right* Way

Isabelle and Dan have been married for eight years. They are arguing over Dan's decision to spend money on a new car he would like to purchase. Isabelle is trying to remain calm because she manages the money and believes they cannot afford a new car at this time. Dan begins to raise his voice at Isabelle as she attempts to explain why the purchase of a new car is not a good idea at this time.

Dan then says to Isabelle in an angry tone, and with an angry expression on his face, "I'm the one who commutes a long distance through traffic every day, and you don't."

Isabelle replies, "I know you're angry right now, but we need to be reasonable."

Dan says back (in a very angry tone), "I'm not angry! I know when I'm angry." Dan then storms out of the room to his office, slamming the door behind him.

Recognizing: Measuring Intensity

Emotions are experienced at various levels of stress ranging from high, to moderate, to low. Stress is the degree of intensity behind the emotion. The higher the intensity behind an emotion, the greater the pressure builds up inside the person experiencing the emotion. This pressure is experienced as tension in the body. The higher the tension levels are in a person's body, the greater the chance the emotion may be acted upon. If the emotion is a negative one, such as anger or fear, the behavior that follows could be harmful.

Another reason for measuring intensity is because a person's ability to think clearly or reasonably is lessened if the intensity in the person's body is too high.

> **RECOGNIZING EMOTIONS** means *accurately*
> *measuring* the *intensity* or level of tension in the
> body and determining if it is high, moderate, or low.

DVD

RECOGNIZING EMOTION: Measuring Intensity
 — The *Wrong* Way and the *Right* Way

Making the Point—The WRONG Way
The Case of Dan's Continuing Dilemma

Dan is now in his office after slamming his door. As he sits down behind his desk, he takes a deep breath, trying to calm down. Isabelle enters his office. She says to Dan, "I'm sorry you're angry about this, but I still believe it's not a good time to buy a new car."

Dan's intensity level is still very high when he says, "I don't want to talk to you right now, so please leave." He continues (in a very critical tone), "Isabelle, I think you are a very selfish person who doesn't appreciate how hard I work. I just want some time to myself, so just leave."

Recognizing: Naming

Once the general category of an emotion is identified and the intensity level is measured (high, moderate, low), the third skill in recognizing emotions is "naming" the emotion. Naming emotions requires a broad vocabulary. The more words you have to describe emotions, the more precise and accurate you will be in naming an emotion.

The ability to accurately and precisely name the emotion(s) you and others are experiencing is essential if you want to successfully manage those emotions. It takes a higher level of thinking ability to come up with precise vocabulary words. This higher level of thinking indicates that you have greater control of your emotions because you are not only feeling, but you are also thinking, *and* you are able to connect your feelings and your thoughts together.

It's important to remember that the more you are able to talk about how you feel, the less likely you are to act on it.

DVD
RECOGNIZING EMOTION: Naming
— The *Wrong* Way and the *Right* Way

Practice

Carefully read the scenario below:

> You and your spouse have been arguing a lot lately about money and expenditures. Your spouse believes that you spend too much on yourself. The two of you also disagree regarding disciplining your children. Recently, you've noticed that your spouse does not speak to you unless spoken to. You've decided that you need to confront him/her on his/her unwillingness to initiate a conversation. An argument ensues, and your spouse says, "I'm having doubts about our relationship. Maybe we need to question our staying together. Every time I ask for understanding regarding the finances, the children, or our relationship, you think you're always right."

Place a check next to the emotions that you think the spouse that just made this statement is feeling:

- ☐ Scared
- ☐ Hurt
- ☐ Fed up
- ☐ Torn
- ☐ Belittled

- ☐ Indifferent
- ☐ Frustrated
- ☐ Furious
- ☐ Forceful
- ☐ Bewildered

See page 142 for our answers.

Making the Point—The RIGHT Way
The Case of Dan's De-escalation

Upon hearing Dan tell her to leave him alone, Isabelle decided to try to calm him down. She started out by saying, "I know you're angry at me. That's obvious." Dan shook his head, acknowledging that he is still angry and, in spite of himself, began to calm down.

Isabelle then asked, "Are you mad?" to which Dan responded, "No."

Isabelle pressed on, "Are you furious?" to which Dan responded, "No."

Isabelle tried again, "Are you annoyed?" to which Dan responded, "No."

Then Dan stated, "I'm offended."

Isabelle acknowledged Dan's statement by saying, "Okay, can you tell me why you're offended?"

Now, the two of them could engage in a meaningful conversation that included respecting and understanding each other's feelings.

How to Be in a Personal Relationship

Action Strategies

Below are some Strategies for Recognizing Emotions you may want to use in your personal relationships if the situation allows for it.

1. The next time your partner comes home at the end of the day:

    *   Look at his/her facial expression.

    *   See if you can identify the category of emotion he/she is expressing through voice tone and/or facial expression.

    *   Then say, "You look/sound _____ (angry, sad, happy, tired)."

    a. After completing the above and getting the emotion category affirmed:

        *   Identify the intensity of the emotions as high, moderate, low.

        *   Then say one of the following:

            "You look/sound *really* (for high) _____ (emotional category)."

            OR

            "You look/sound *somewhat* (for moderate) _____ (emotional category)."

            OR

            "You look/sound *a little* (for low) _____ (emotional category)."

    b. After completing the above and getting the category and the intensity affirmed, pick a feeling word that is more precise that reflects that category and intensity.

        *   Then say: "You look/sound _____ (correct emotion word for category and intensity)."

2. The next time you are experiencing an emotion that's causing you tension, do the following steps:

    *   Identify the category: _____

    *   Identify the intensity level (high, moderate, low): _____

    *   Identify a feeling word that captures both the category and the intensity: _____

3. While having dinner with your partner, you notice he/she is in a good mood or really enjoying the occasion. At the appropriate time, go through the three steps for identifying emotions:

- Identify category: _____ (e.g., happy)

- Identify intensity: _____ (e.g., moderate)

- Identify feeling word: _____ (e.g., pleased)

Now, write a Recognizing Emotion Action Strategy:

_____

_____

_____

_____

_____

Reasoning

Emotions, especially intense ones, can often dampen—or even para-lyze—our ability to reason. This is why some cultures support the suppression of emotion.

Reasoning is the ability to think in rational terms. It requires skill in processing our thoughts so that the actions that follow are in our best interest and, if others are involved, in the best interests of others. Reasoning involves considering all the facts before making a rational decision. This means getting as much relevant information as possible from as many different sources as possible. This is one of those times when lots of heads are better than one if your goal is to make the best possible rational decision.

Unfortunately, there are, and will be, many instances when we do not have sufficient knowledge or skills available to us to make the best decision. Sometimes, in these situations, we may begin to become emotional as a coping mechanism. If we allow our emotions to take over, we may even act impulsively.

There are three sub-skills to Reasoning: Attributing, Externalizing, and Internalizing.

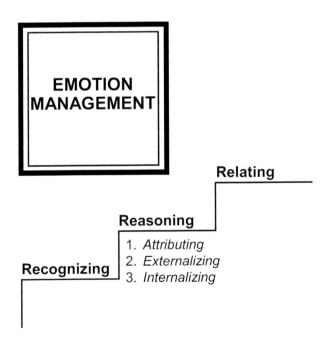

Ramona hasn't dated very much in her life because she is on the fast track to becoming a lawyer. Ramona breezed through her four years of college in three years. Then she was accepted into a prestigious law school at age 20. She is in her second year of law school.

Recently, Ramona met a young man named Ron. Ron is the first man she has met that she has felt an interest in. Unfortunately, Ramona is not knowledgeable or skilled at relationships. She dated some in high school but never had a steady boyfriend.

Ramona and Ron went out to dinner one evening. Just as their dinner was served, a woman, who happened to be a former girlfriend of Ron's, saw Ron and approached him to say hello. This ex-girlfriend still had feelings for Ron. As the ex-girlfriend approached Ron, she said, "Hello," but then she completely ignored Ramona. Ron appeared nervous at seeing his ex-girlfriend. After a few social pleasantries, the ex-girlfriend started to walk away. She then turned back and said to Ron, "Why don't you give me a call sometime?" Ron responded, "Sure."

Ramona is now fuming inside. She has become quiet. Ron doesn't say anything about the ex-girlfriend. He asks Ramona if she is enjoying her meal. Ramona doesn't say anything. Ron then asks, "Are you all right?" to which Ramona responds, "Fine," and says nothing else.

Ron continues to eat, but he also keeps trying to engage Ramona in conversation. Ramona doesn't respond but finally says, "I'd like to go home now." When Ron attempts to ask what's wrong, Ramona says, "Nothing. I just want to go home."

Ron takes Ramona home. There is total silence during the ride home. Ramona gets out of Ron's car and says nothing. Then, she enters her apartment. Ron drives off confused because he doesn't understand why Ramona's whole mood changed.

We will revisit Ramona and Ron's situation because it reflects what happens when the reasoning techniques are not considered when managing emotions.

Reasoning: Attributing

Attributing is the ability to determine the cause or causes of the emotions you and/or another person are experiencing. In other words, it is an attempt to attribute our feelings to some*thing* or some*one*.

Let's look back at Ron and Ramona's situation. Is Ramona attributing her anger to Ron, to Ron's ex-girlfriend, or to herself? To determine the answer to this question, Ramona might say to herself, "I have this feeling. Now, what's causing it?"

Attributing is important because it helps a person understand the reasons behind their emotions. It requires people to begin to think about their emotions after they have identified them.

> **REASONING** means *attributing* correctly
> in order to determine the cause or causes
> of an emotion.

 DVD

REASONING: Attributing
— The *Wrong* Way and the *Right* Way

Practice

Write down three possible reasons for Ramona's anger.

Example: Ron's saying "Sure" when the ex-girlfriend says to call her sometime.

1. _____

_____

2. _____

_____

3. _____

_____

The Case of Ron and Ramona's Rocky Dinner: Part II

Ramona and Ron have not spoken in a few days because she will not take his calls. Ramona is angry at Ron because she believes (attributes) Ron's telling his ex-girlfriend "Sure" when she asks him to call her sometime indicates he is still interested in her. What Ramona is unaware of is that Ron said, "Sure," to get his ex-girlfriend to leave.

Ron's relationship with his ex-girlfriend was volatile. He broke it off with her because she was always losing her temper with him if she couldn't get her own way. He thought by saying, "Sure," the ex-girlfriend would leave and not cause a scene.

Ramona is also hurt because Ron never told her about his ex-girlfriend, and he didn't even introduce her when she came to the table. Ramona was hurt because she believed (attributed) Ron's actions were rude and inconsiderate.

In reality, Ron did not introduce his ex-girlfriend because he was shocked and uneasy about seeing her in the restaurant. He also didn't introduce Ramona to his ex-girlfriend because he didn't want the ex-girlfriend to know Ramona's name. He was fearful the ex-girlfriend might be a threat to Ramona. Ron had been getting a lot of anonymous phone calls lately, and he thinks it might be his ex-girlfriend. Ron was also nervous because he felt his ex-girlfriend is capable of stalking him, and she may have followed him to the restaurant.

Reasoning: Externalizing

When we experience intense emotions, especially negative ones, we tend to place the cause of these feelings onto people or events outside of ourselves. Externalizing our emotions, or blaming our emotions, on things outside ourselves is less threatening to us. The reason for this may be because we don't have to take responsibility for how we feel if we believe we are not the cause.

For example, it's fairly common for people to **not** want to take credit for their actions when their actions generate negative outcomes, just as it's fairly common for people to want to take credit when their actions generate positive outcomes. By refusing to take credit for negative outcomes, we can also avoid the negative feelings we may have toward ourselves.

Of course, there are events or people in our lives outside of our control that can cause us to experience emotions within ourselves. Being disappointed about not getting the promotion we wanted; being sad that a loved one is seriously ill; experiencing grief if that loved one dies; being angry because someone has stolen something from you—all of these are good examples of events and people over whom we have no control that create deep emotions in us.

The key to the externalizing skill, as well as the internalizing skill that we will discuss next, is the ability to objectively attribute the causes for your emotions.

> **REASONING** means accurately *externalizing by* objectively attributing the cause of your emotion to people or events outside of your control.

DVD

REASONING: Externalizing
— The *Wrong* Way and the *Right* Way

Practice

Write down two emotions Ron may be experiencing regarding Ramona and what external attributes he's basing them on.

Example: *annoyed* because Ramona is immature

1. Emotion: _____ because (external attribution) _____

   _____

2. Emotion: _____ because (external attribution) _____

   _____

Think back to an experience in your life where you became angry at someone. Write down what caused (attributed) your feelings and if you externalized the responsibility for them.

1. Experience: _____

   _____

2. Emotion felt: _____

3. What caused your emotion: _____

   _____

Ramona will not accept Ron's attempts to reach her by phone or return his e-mails. She believes she has a right to be angry because of his behavior at the restaurant. In other words, she is blaming Ron for her anger and being hurt.

Ron has had time to think about Ramona's anger toward him. Initially, from the time he left the restaurant until the next day, he was confused by her behavior. He also became angry with Ramona when his initial attempts to contact her did not work.

On the third day following the restaurant incident, Ron started to modify his feelings toward Ramona. He realized that Ramona had a right to be angry at him because he didn't explain the reasons for his actions.

Ron is now beginning to feel guilty (internalizing his emotions), because he understands that if the circumstances were reversed, he would be angry. He decides to write Ramona an e-mail explaining his behavior at dinner.

Reasoning: Internalizing

It is very difficult for us to take responsibility for our emotions, especially when they are negative. We want to vent them or expel them from our bodies. As a matter of fact, suppressing them can actually be physically painful. Internalizing your emotions can initially cause a suppressing sensation in your body. We are not suggesting that you suppress your emotions by learning to internalize.

Internalizing is the ability to separate the responsibility for the emotions you are experiencing at any given time. It is asking the question, "Is there something I am doing/not doing or thinking/not thinking that is causing me to feel the way I feel?" It is also asking the question, "If I am feeling this way (e.g., angry, anxious, sad) due to some external cause, how can I regulate it so that it doesn't cause harm to myself or others?"

> **REASONING** means accurately *internalizing* by objectively attributing the responsibility for your emotion to yourself—either due to your own actions or due to how you choose to *feel* about something that has happened *to* you.

REASONING: Internalizing
— The *Wrong* Way and the *Right* Way

Practice

Think back to an experience in your life involving a personal relationship where you emotionally overreacted. Write down what happened:

_____

_____

_____

_____

Now, if you could revisit that experience and internalize your emotional reactions, how could it have improved the outcome?

_____

_____

_____

_____

_____

Making the Point—The RIGHT Way
The Case of Ron and Ramona's Rocky Dinner: Part IV

Ron is beginning to accept emotional responsibility for his behavior at dinner with Ramona. Initially, he was feeling confused as to why she was acting cold toward him. Then he became somewhat angry with her because she was refusing to take his calls or respond to his e-mails. Ron's emotions toward Ramona at that time were due to his not looking at his behavior at dinner with his ex-girlfriend while with Ramona. Nor was he thinking how he might feel toward Ramona if an ex-boyfriend had approached them at dinner, and she had acted the same way he did.

Ron is now internalizing his emotions. He is feeling stupid because he couldn't see how his actions caused Ramona to be upset with him. He is also feeling guilty because he understands why Ramona is upset with him.

Ramona has also had time to think about her emotional reactions toward Ron. She decides to read Ron's e-mail where he explains his actions. As she reads Ron's e-mail, she starts to feel bad because she now realizes why he acted the way he did.

(continued)

Ramona is beginning to internalize her emotions now that she realizes her perceptions (thinking) of Ron's behavior were based on incorrect assumptions. Her emotional reactions were, therefore, incorrect. She also accepts that her lack of dating experience may have caused her to jump to conclusions. She tells herself she was really feeling jealous, and this is what made her angry at Ron.

Action Strategies

Below are some Reasoning Strategies you may want to use in your personal relationships if the situation allows for it.

The next time you have a disagreement with a loved one that caused you to be angry, write down all the possible causes (attributions) for your anger.

a. Now, put a checkmark next to the ones that indicate that you placed the responsibility onto the other person (externalized ones).

- Now, write down the feelings you had when you externalized the causes for your emotions.

b. Now, look at the possible causes for your anger that you recorded that *you* may be responsible for.

- Now write down the feelings you had toward yourself when you internalized the causes.

Now, write a Reasoning Action Strategy:

_____

_____

_____

_____

_____

Relating

Relating is the ability to constructively express our emotions toward others. It is also the ability to receive the emotions that others convey to us in a constructive manner. The constructive expression and reception of emotion requires the skills discussed in the Nonverbal and Mental Attending sections of this book. It also requires verbal skills discussed in the next section.

The constructive expression and reception of emotions is the glue for maintaining the positive feelings (love, empathy, respect, genuineness) that are the foundation for personal relationships. That's not to say that there won't be negative feelings in our personal relationships. Those are inevitable, and they also need to be regulated, expressed, and received in constructive ways so that they do not destroy the relationship.

There are three sub-skills to Relating: Regulating, Expressing Emotions, and Receiving the Emotions from Others.

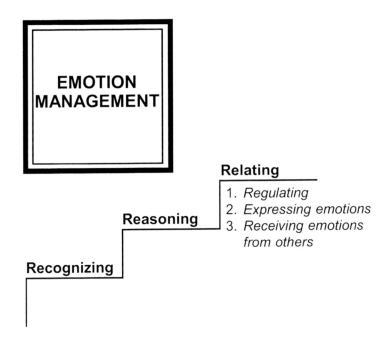

EMOTION MANAGEMENT

Relating
1. *Regulating*
2. *Expressing emotions*
3. *Receiving emotions from others*

Reasoning

Recognizing

Relating: Regulating

Regulating requires the skills of Recognizing and Reasoning discussed previously. Regulating is processing your emotions by recognizing what you are feeling and the intensity behind it. Recognizing begins the process of thinking about emotions before expressing them. Thinking about emotions increases control of those emotions.

Once you have recognized the emotion, you move to the reasoning stage. Reasoning helps you process all the possible causes (attributions) for your emotions. It also helps you place the appropriate responsibility for your emotion onto external and/or internal reasons. It starts the process of taking responsibility for your emotions before you express them.

Regulating is also the ability to maintain the Nonverbal Attending and Mental Attending skills discussed earlier as you begin to express or receive the emotions of others. It is the ability to tell yourself how you are going to act once you have identified your emotions and reasoned out the causes for those emotions. You do this by telling yourself that you are going to nonverbally attend (arranging, positioning, posturing, gesturing, facing, vocalizing) when you express your emotions and the reasons for these emotions as well as when you receive the other persons' reactions. It also means you are going to mentally attend carefully to the other person using your visual and listening skills while you are expressing your thoughts and feelings as well as receiving their thoughts and feelings.

The goal of regulating is the modeling of self-control when managing your emotions and the emotions of others.

> **RELATING** means *regulating*, or using your nonverbal and mental attending skills along with your emotion recognition and reasoning skills to model self-control when managing your emotions or the emotions of others.

DVD

RELATING: Regulating
— The *Wrong* Way and the *Right* Way

Practice

Write down an experience that you had with a loved one when taking the time to regulate yourself could have helped.

_____

_____

_____

_____

_____

Making the Point—The WRONG Way
The Case of Adam the Avoider

Angela and Adam have been married for 25 years. They have what others would describe as a committed relationship. They have two children—one in college and one about to finish high school.

Recently, Angela has been feeling restless. Prior to having children, Angela was on the fast track in her career. She was getting one promotion after another at work. However, when Angela became pregnant with their first child, she decided she wanted to become a full-time parent for her children. Adam was fine with that and said he would work extra jobs if necessary to compensate for the financial changes due to the loss of Angela's income.

Now that their youngest child is about to go to college, Angela would like to go back to work full-time and see if she can resume her prior successes vocationally. Angela decides to have an open discussion with Adam about her plans. The last couple of times she's hinted to Adam that she was thinking about going back to work, he appeared uneasy and said he didn't want to talk about it.

It is now Tuesday evening and none of the children are home. Angela decides to have dinner on the porch with Adam. After dinner, they both clean the kitchen, and Angela asks Adam to sit down with her on the porch. She starts out by saying she wants to discuss her going back to work full-time. As she does, Adam says he doesn't want to talk about it. Adam then becomes angry, stands up, and begins to walk in the kitchen. Angela follows him, attempting to keep the conversation going. Adam then says, "I don't want to talk about it."

Angela asks, "Are you angry?"

Adam responds, in an angry tone, "I'm not angry, so drop it," and then says, "I'm going for a walk."

Relating: Expressing Emotions

Expressing is the ability to tell another person what you are feeling and why you feel it. It is also the ability to accept the possibility that your feelings and attributions may be incorrect based on the feedback you get from the other person.

It's important to keep in mind that you may not have the time to take a walk or a "time out" when someone says or does something that upsets you or catches you off guard. A good strategy in this situation is to be quiet, suppress your emotions momentarily, and let them continue to talk.

There are also some helpful verbal techniques (responding) that will be discussed later in the book. These verbal techniques, when used along with your nonverbal and mental attending skills, will help you when you feel emotionally provoked by another person's words or actions.

> **RELATING** means *expressing emotions*
> appropriately by telling another person what
> you are feeling and why.

DVD

RELATING: Expressing Emotions
— The *Wrong* Way and the *Right* Way

Practice

Write about a time when you were involved in an emotionally heated discussion with a loved one and didn't use expressing skills.

_____

_____

_____

_____

_____

Now write what you should have said using the skills discussed above if you could do it over again.

_____

_____

_____

_____

_____

Making the Point—The RIGHT Way
The Case of Adam's Comeback

Adam has gone back to the house to talk with Angela. He has decided to regulate his emotions while also expressing his concerns.

Adam tells Angela he would like to go back out to the porch (*arranging*) and discuss the situation. He asks Angela to sit in a chair directly across from him and about three feet away (*positioning*). He maintains an erect posture with a slight forward lean toward Angela (*posturing*). He puts his hands in his lap and decides to keep his body still (*gesturing*). He tells himself to keep his facial expressions neutral while Angela speaks (*facing*). He tells himself, "*I will also keep my voice tone in control* (*vocalizing*) *as much as possible.*"

Adam then begins to express to Angela why he is reacting to her going back to work. He tells her that he's angry, and then he explains why he is angry. He tells her he is uneasy about her going back to work, and then tells her why. He finishes up his conversation by telling her he is feeling a little threatened by her desire to return to work, and then he tells her why.

Angela listens very carefully without reacting to Adam's perceptions. She practices good nonverbal and mental attending while Adam expresses his concerns.

Once he has finished talking, Adam prepares himself to listen to Angela using his skills because he knows it's important for Angela to express her views and emotions regarding the situation.

Relating: Receiving Emotions from Others

Receiving is the ability to constructively hear what another person is feeling and thinking while maintaining good nonverbal and mental attending skills. It is also the ability to regulate your internal thoughts and emotional processing while listening to another person, especially if what they have to say is negative or provoking. Receiving takes a lot of self-control.

The main goal of receiving is to keep the other person's verbal and emotional expressions from causing you to react negatively, possibly resulting in an escalated conflict.

A second goal of receiving is to set the tone for the expression of your thoughts and feelings. If you are emotionally receptive when the other person's thoughts and feelings are expressed, there is a greater chance they will return the favor and be emotionally receptive when it's your turn to express your views.

> **RELATING** means *receiving emotions* from others by attending to what another person is feeling and saying.

 DVD

RELATING: Receiving Emotions from Others — The *Wrong* Way and the *Right* Way

Practice

Describe a time when you did **not** do a good job receiving what a loved one had to say and it made the situation worse.

_____

_____

_____

_____

_____

Now write what you should have said using the skills discussed above if you could do it over again.

_____

_____

_____

_____

_____

How to Be in a Personal Relationship

Adam has finished expressing his views to Angela about her returning to the workplace, and Angela has shown a lot of patience while he spoke. Now it's Angela's turn, and Adam has prepared himself to receive what she has to say.

Angela starts out by saying, "Adam, I feel *appreciative* (*recognize*) when I think how hard you have worked so that I could be a full-time parent (*reasoning*). I feel *fortunate* (*recognize*) because you were a husband who understood how important it was for me to be a stay-at-home mom. I felt *guilty* (*recognize*) when I realized that most families had two incomes because the wife worked, and I could have taken the financial pressure off you (*reasoning*). I feel *confident* (*recognize*) that my working will not change our lifestyles in a negative way; in fact it might allow you to retire early. And finally, there is no way I would ever be interested in someone else. I feel *so confident* (*recognize*) in my choice of marrying you (*reasoning*)".

Adam was overwhelmed and so glad he practiced emotional management skills in handling his fears.

Action Strategies

Below are some Relating Strategies you may want to use in your personal relationships if the situation allows for it.

The next time you experience an intense emotion due to a partner's words or actions, **identify what they are feeling and identify what you are feeling.**

a. After identifying their emotions and your emotions, **determine the reason(s) for their emotions and the reason(s) for your emotions.**

b. Now say to them, *"It sounds like you are feeling _____ (feeling word) because _____ (state the reason for their emotion)."* Maintain your nonverbal and mental attending skills while stating the above.

c. If they acknowledge that you have identified their feelings and the reasons for them correctly, say the following, *"I feel _____ (feeling word) because _____ (reason[s] for your feelings)."* Maintain your nonverbal and mental attending skills while stating the above.

d. Now repeat steps a through c if your partner begins to convey more information and reveals more of the feelings they are experiencing. Use the following model as an example:

Your partner says, *"I don't like it when you keep interrupting me when I try to talk. Why can't you just listen?"*

Identify your partner's feeling as **"aggravated."**
Identify your feeling as **"stunned."**

Now, you can say to your partner, *"You're feeling aggravated with me because I have this bad habit of interrupting you before you finish."*

Your partner may say, *"Yes."*

You can then say, *"I'm feeling stunned, because I was completely unaware that I was doing that to you. I'm sorry."*

Your partner may say, *"I didn't realize you weren't aware of it. I guess I just assumed you knew you were doing it."*

Now, write a Relating Action Strategy:

_____
_____
_____
_____
_____

How to Be in a Personal Relationship

Skills Summary
Emotion Management

Now let's review all of the skills and sub-skills involved in Emotion Management.

EMOTION MANAGEMENT

Relating
1. *Regulating*
2. *Expressing emotions*
3. *Receiving emotions from others*

Reasoning
1. *Attributing*
2. *Externalizing*
3. *Internalizing*

Recognizing
1. *Categorizing*
2. *Measuring intensity*
3. *Naming*

Answers to Recognizing Emotion: Naming Practice on p. 122

You and your spouse have been arguing a lot lately about money and expenditures. Your spouse believes that you spend too much on yourself. The two of you also disagree regarding disciplining your children. Recently, you've noticed that your spouse does not speak to you unless spoken to. You've decided that you need to confront him/her on his/her unwillingness to initiate a conversation. An argument ensues, and your spouse says, "I'm having doubts about our relationship. Maybe we need to question our staying together. Every time I ask for understanding regarding the finances, the children, or our relationship, you think you're always right."

Place a check next to the emotions that you think the spouse that just made this statement is feeling.

☐ Scared	☐ Indifferent
☑ Hurt	☑ Frustrated
☑ Fed up	☐ Furious
☑ Torn	☑ Forceful
☑ Belittled	☐ Bewildered

So, how did you do? If you didn't match our answers, that's okay. Remember, you are completing this practice using only one of your senses—your vision. In other words, you only have the benefit of *reading* this scenario. You don't know the circumstances that led up to this conversation. You don't know the people involved. You can't observe their gestures and facial displays. The important thing is for you to become aware of how powerful naming emotions can be.

How to Be in a Personal Relationship

Section III

Verbal Communication

We are a talking species—we value language and the use of words. We are taught at a very early age to hear, speak, read, and write words. We use them to communicate our thoughts, feelings, and needs. A major component of human intelligence is based on a person's vocabulary. In other words, we tend to judge how intelligent a person is based on how large their vocabulary is. The bottom line is that when we talk to people, we use words. Unfortunately, having a broad vocabulary doesn't ensure social success in human interactions.

Besides the words themselves, there are verbal techniques necessary to accomplish your relationship goals. A verbal technique is how to say something beyond the words themselves. An analogy would be the throwing of a baseball or softball using a certain technique when you release the ball. The pitcher cradles the ball in his or her hand in different ways such that, when the ball is thrown, it follows different paths (e.g., fast ball, change up, curve ball). These different paths, or the delivery of the ball, represent the technique.

When we talk with others, the techniques, as well as the words, are critical in determining the outcome.

Making the Point—The RIGHT Way
The Case of Rosa's Responsible Responding

Rosa and Mica are discussing a problem they are having with their children. Below is their dialogue as they discuss the problem. After each statement, you will see the technique used in parentheses.

Rosa: What am I doing wrong that I get this flip reaction from you lately whenever I ask you to do something? *(asking a question)*

Mica: I've been having trouble at work with my new boss, and I guess I'm on edge because of it. *(self-disclosing)*

Rosa: You're saying that you have a new boss, and you're having trouble with him. I didn't know you had a new boss. *(responding)*

Mica: Yeah. I get so frustrated because he is constantly critical of my work. *(self-disclosure)*

(continued)

Rosa:	You've got to be anxious with all the downsizing going on in the company. *(responding to meaning)*
Mica:	Would you mind if we didn't talk about this now because I gotta call him (the new boss)? He just left me a text message. I better call him. *(making a request)*
Rosa:	Sure, I understand. We can talk later. *(handling a request)*
Mica:	I really appreciate your patience with me lately. *(reinforcing using a positive verbal reinforcer)*

In the above scenario, several verbal techniques were utilized by Rosa and Mica. The use of these techniques (asking questions, responding, self-disclosing, making and handling requests, and reinforcing) enabled Rosa and Mica to successfully manage a stressful situation.

In this section of the book, we will be discussing each of the verbal techniques discussed above as skills associated with effective verbal communication. Verbal Communication comprises three important components: Rapport Building, Intimacy Building, and Managing Skills.

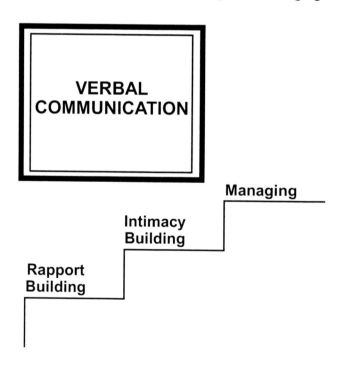

How to Be in a Personal Relationship

Rapport Building

Our needs are more likely to be met by those we have rapport with. Rapport is basically a measure of how well two people get along with each other. Rapport can be measured by the amount of positive interaction as opposed to negative interaction that occurs between people.

Rapport Building is critical to relationship success and maintenance. When two people have rapport, the communication is open, efficient, and effective, and stress levels are reduced.

Relationships that lack rapport are difficult to be in. They take a lot of energy to maintain, and it is often an "uphill battle" just to get your basic needs met with the relationship. These relationships are often characterized by criticisms, power struggles, threats, manipulative behaviors, and, sometimes, no verbal communication at all.

Rapport can be viewed like the oil in a car engine or the grease on a car's axle. Without the oil or grease, you have metal rubbing on metal. This causes intense heat and friction, and eventually this will result in damage to the metal—and expensive car repairs! Without rapport, a couple may find themselves embroiled in a lot of tension and friction, and the result might be a relationship that is heavily damaged, and maybe even destroyed.

The goal of rapport-building skills is to keep the heat, or friction, in the relationship to a minimum between you and your partner and prevent further damage.

The sub-skills of Rapport Building are Responding Techniques based on Content, Feeling, and Meaning, and Asking Relevant Questions.

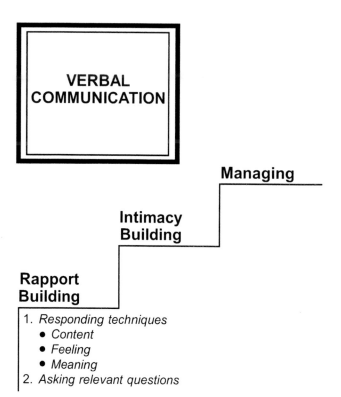

VERBAL COMMUNICATION

Managing

Intimacy Building

Rapport Building

1. *Responding techniques*
   - *Content*
   - *Feeling*
   - *Meaning*
2. *Asking relevant questions*

Rapport Building: Responding Techniques

Responding is a set of verbal techniques that facilitate rapport between people. Responding is rapport building because it is a demonstration of a clear reaction to something that you have seen or heard. Responding **gives evidence** that you are paying attention, you are observing, and you are listening.

In this section, we will take a look at several levels of responding. At the simplest level, you can **respond to content** by summarizing and expressing what a person has said or done. At the next level, you can respond to the **feelings** shown in a person's words or reflected in his actions. The third step in responding is conveying the reasons for those feelings, or the **meaning**.

Each new level of responding does more to show a person that you are really on top of things—really seeing, hearing, and understanding him or her in terms of where he or she is. Probably more than anything else, responding may seem strange to you. It's new, and you may be doubtful about its worth. There are some things to remember here:

- We are not telling you that you can't use other communication techniques that have worked for you in the past.

- We *are* trying to "add-on" to techniques you may already have in order to increase your communication abilities.

- The more techniques you have to handle a given situation in life, the greater your chances of success and/or control of the outcome. Techniques are like tools in a toolbox—the more tools you have and the more you know how to use them, the greater the chance you have of fixing a problem.

Responding to Content. Responding to content refers to the ability to see and hear what is really happening and then be able to reflect that understanding back to a person. When you are able to reflect your interpretation of the context back to the person accurately, you are letting that person know that you heard accurately, and you are on top of the situation.

While your use of the nonverbal and mental attending techniques establishes a relationship with people so that they will be more likely to cooperate with and talk to you, your use of responding allows you to be more spontaneous in your communication with others. Responding to content is the first part of effective responding. When a person knows that you are seeing and/or hearing him or her accurately, he or she will tend to talk more freely. This is critical because talking not only gives you more of the information you need, it also allows people to get things "off their chests."

There are two steps to Responding to Content (1) Reflecting on what was seen and heard, and (2) Using the Responding Format to respond to content.

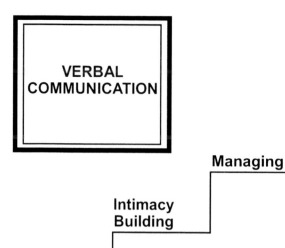

VERBAL COMMUNICATION

Managing

Intimacy Building

Rapport Building

1. *Responding techniques*
   - *Content*
     - *Reflect on what was seen and heard*
     - *Use a responding format to respond to content*
   - *Feeling*
   - *Meaning*
2. *Asking relevant questions*

When responding to content, you are focused on what your partner is either saying or doing. Using what you have learned, you focus on arranging your environment, posturing, positioning, gesturing, facing, vocalizing, and appearing. Next, you reflect on what you have seen and heard: "What is he/she doing?" "What is he/she saying?" "How does he/she look?" In answering these questions, pay close attention to what is actually going on and/or what is being said.

Finally, after taking it all in and reflecting on it, you summarize what your partner is saying or doing in your own words. You respond to the content by saying to a person either:

"You look (it looks)_____."

OR

"You're saying _____."

For example, "You **look** pretty busy," or "You're **saying** you are pretty busy."

You respond to content when you want more information. You may want to do this when you are just talking with a person, or maybe you want to use this skill when you notice unusual behavior in a person, and you would like to get some information from them about what they are doing. For example, you might notice your partner is very quiet. You could say to them, "You're pretty quiet today." This gives them the opportunity to respond to you while it communicates to the person that you are observing them accurately. Unlike other approaches designed to get information, responding to content doesn't automatically put people on the defensive.

> **RESPONDING** at the simplest level reflects content:
> "You're saying _____."

 DVD

**RAPPORT BUILDING: Responding to Content
— The *Wrong* Way and the *Right* Way**

Practice

List two examples of situations in which you might respond to content in order to get more information from your partner.

Example: Your partner seems to be "down" about something.

1. _____

_____

2. _____

_____

List two reasons why you might want to respond to content.

Example: When your partner is "down" and it affects your relationship with him/her.

1. _____

_____

2. _____

_____

Joy and Nolan have been dating for about a year. It's Saturday evening, and Nolan has just arrived at Joy's apartment. They have a dinner and movie date. As Nolan enters Joy's apartment, he observes that Joy is not ready in terms of her appearance. This is abnormal or unlike her based on her appearance. Joy looks stressed to Nolan, and he says, "You look stressed. Are you okay?"

Joy responds that she has just gotten off the phone with her mother. Her mother had told her that Joy's dad has been complaining about not feeling well, but he won't go to the doctor. Joy's dad had a heart attack about a year ago but doesn't like doctors or hospitals.

Nolan responds, "You're saying that your mom is worried about your dad, and now you're concerned."

Joy says, "Yes."

Nolan then says, "Why don't we skip the dinner and movie and go by your parents' house?"

Joy says, "Okay, I appreciate you saying that. I'm sorry about the dinner and movie."

Nolan responds, "No problem."

Responding to Feeling. Responding to feeling is the ability to capture in words the specific "feeling experience" being presented by your partner. By responding to, or reflecting back, the partner's feeling, you show that you understand that feeling. This encourages your partner to talk and release his or her feelings.

The two steps in Responding to Feeling are (1) Reflect on feeling and (2) Reflect on feeling and intensity.

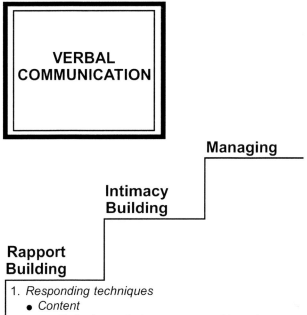

VERBAL COMMUNICATION

Managing

Intimacy Building

Rapport Building

1. *Responding techniques*
   - *Content*
     - *Reflect on what was seen and heard*
     - *Use a responding format to respond to content*
   - *Feeling*
     - *Reflect on feeling*
     - *Reflect on feeling and intensity*
   - *Meaning*
2. *Asking relevant questions*

Everyone has feelings that affect what they say and do. The nature and strength of these feelings usually determine what they are going to do. When you respond to a partner's feelings, you are encouraging him or her to talk. The skill of responding to feelings has important implications for the emotional health of your relationship.

Showing that you understand how your partner feels can be more powerful than showing that you understand the content of their actions and/or words. Showing a partner that you understand their negative feelings can usually **defuse** those negative feelings. By responding to feelings at the verbal, or "symbolic," behavior level, you keep the partner's words from turning into action. Also, responding to feelings at a verbal level can give you the necessary clues to determine a person's intentions. If your partner "clams up" after you have responded to his/her feelings, he/she may be telling you that he/she is going to act on those intentions. On the other hand, if your partner engages you verbally, that may be their way of telling you that he/she wants to talk it out instead of *act* on it.

Besides being able to defuse negative feelings so that negative words don't become negative actions, responding to feelings leads to greater understanding. And, when you respond to positive feelings, these feelings get reinforced (unlike negative feelings). There's nothing mysterious about this. We don't enjoy our negative feelings, so we get rid of them by sharing them—by talking them out. But we do enjoy our positive feelings, so they only become stronger when they're shared with another person. You can choose to strengthen the positive feelings that will help a partner act more positively simply by recognizing and responding to these feelings. As a general rule, a person who feels positive about him- or herself will try to do positive things, while a person who feels negative about him- or herself will try to do negative things. If you expand on this, you arrive at the general principle: **People tend to act in ways consistent with the way other significant people see and act toward them.**

RESPONDING at the next level reflects feelings:
"You feel _____."

Practice

List two situations where it would be important and useful to defuse negative feelings of a partner.

Example: Your partner did not get the job promotion they really wanted.

1. _____

_____

2. _____

_____

Making the Point—The WRONG Way
The Case of Jacob the Insensitive Jerk

Jane and Jacob are engaged to be married. Jane is reluctant to get married to Jacob because she, as well as some of her family and friends, has noticed that Jacob is often selfish about wanting his way.

Recently, Jane received a call from her older sister who lives in another state. Her sister wanted to know if Jane and Jacob would like to visit her for a weekend. Jane's sister has a home on the beach, and it is a beautiful place to visit. Besides enjoying her sister's home, Jane is very close to her sister.

It is now Wednesday night, and Jane decides to ask Jacob about visiting her sister. She is very excited about seeing her sister and going to the beach. Jacob is watching television when she approaches him. She says, "Jacob, I've got some really good news. My sister has asked us to come to the beach for a few days. I would really love to go."

Jacob keeps watching TV and says, "Look, can we talk later? I'm watching the game."

Jane then says, in a pleasant voice, "Jacob, do you want to go? I think it would be fun for us."

Jacob responds, "Look, you're starting to bug me. I don't want to talk about it."

Jane then walks away, gets her things, and leaves Jacob's apartment, slamming the door behind her. Jacob pays no attention. After watching the game, he calls Jane. He says, "What's bugging you?" Jane responds, "You! You're an insensitive jerk. The engagement is off. The engagement ring is on the kitchen counter. Don't call me."

For responding to feeling, you nonverbally attend, then observe and listen. Then you reflect on the feeling (e.g., happy, sad, angry, scared, etc.) and its intensity (e.g., high, medium, or low). Finally, you respond by saying, "You feel _____," for example, "You feel angry."

Here, the new skill involves reflecting on the intensity of the feeling. Adding a new skill doesn't mean discarding the old skills, of course. When trying to determine the intensity of the feeling, you are really asking yourself, "Given what I see and hear, how does my partner basically feel? Is he/she happy, angry, sad, scared?" The person's behaviors and words will let you make a good guess at the feeling. Imagine that your partner shouts at you, "You shouldn't have said that! Now look what you've done!" while shaking his or her head and getting red in the face. In this case, your partner is obviously feeling a level of anger.

After you have picked out a feeling word, you must reflect on the intensity of the feeling. For example, anger can be high in intensity (mad), medium in intensity (annoyed), or low in intensity (bothered). The more accurate your feeling word reflects the intensity, the more effective your response will be—your response will be more accurate and will accomplish your goals more effectively (e.g., defuse the negative feeling). You wouldn't choose *concerned* for the above example because the term would be too weak to describe a person who is yelling, shaking his or her head, and turning red. Such an understatement would probably only make that person angrier. But, "You feel *mad*" would fit just fine.

DVD

| RAPPORT BUILDING: Responding to Feeling
— The *Wrong* Way and the *Right* Way |

Practice

Here is an exercise to improve your emotional vocabulary. The first column lists the seven basic emotions. The following three columns identify the three different intensity levels. Place two words in each cell that are appropriate for both the category of emotion and the intensity level. For example, a high intensity word for happy might be *jubilant*; a moderate intensity word might by *joyful*; a low intensity word might be *fine*. For more of a challenge, time yourself!

Category of Emotion	High Intensity	Moderate Intensity	Low Intensity
Happy			
Sad			
Scared			
Angry			
Confused			
Strong			
Weak			

See pages 208 - 209 for our list of words.

How to Be in a Personal Relationship

Responding to Meaning. Responding to Meaning combines the skills of responding to content and responding to feeling. It requires you to paraphrase the content of a partner's statement is such a way as to provide a meaningful reason for the partner's feeling.

The two steps in Responding to Meaning are (1) Reflect on the feeling and the reason for that feeling and (2) Respond to the feeling and the meaning.

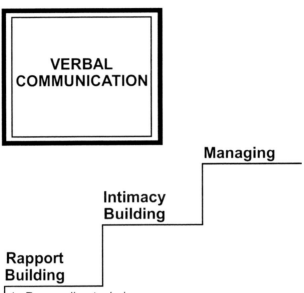

Learning how to respond to content and how to respond to feeling has prepared you to respond to feeling and meaning. Your response at this new level can put everything together. Here, you will effectively capture where your partner is at the moment. By adding the meaning to the feeling, you will help yourself and your partner to understand the reason for his or her feelings about the situation. The reason is simply the personal meaning for that partner.

Chandra and Umberto have been married for five years. They have been trying to have a child for the past two years. They recently saw a fertility specialist who suggested that they consider fertility treatments. The treatment is very expensive and not covered by their health insurance.

They have just arrived home from their appointment with the fertility specialist. During the ride home, they were both cordial toward each other, but there was definitely tension in the air.

During dinner, they again were cordial, saying nothing about the fertility doctor's recommendation. Finally, the following conversation unfolded:

Umberto: Chandra, you haven't said anything about the doctor's recommendation. *(responding to content)*

Chandra: I don't know what we should do.

Umberto: You're feeling unsure. *(responding to feeling)*

Chandra: Yeah, I think I'm responsible for this.

Umberto: You're feeling guilty. *(responding to feeling)*

Chandra: I feel bad because the doctor said your sperm count is fine.

Umberto: You're feeling bad because you believe that the reason for us not having a child is all your fault. *(responding to feeling and meaning)*

Chandra: Yes, and now we might have to spend all this money that we really don't have to spend.

Umberto: So you're also feeling anxious because of the financial strain this situation will put on us. *(responding to feeling and meaning)*

Chandra: Yes, and it's not fair to you. You already work an extra job. (Umberto is a police officer and works a second job 20 hours per week.)

Umberto: It's going to be all right. We can make it work.

In the above example, by putting together the feeling and the meaning and responding to both, Umberto shows that he understands his wife's experience as she presents it. This increases the chances of her talking to him.

By building on what you know, you add the reason to the feeling response you have just learned. Your new way of responding becomes, "You feel _____ because _____."

What we need to focus on here, of course, is an individual's reason (personal meaning) for his or her feeling. Supplying the reason means that you must understand why the event that happened is important. You do this by rephrasing the content in your own words to capture that importance.

Responding is a powerful skill because people feel that you really understand when you respond appropriately. The skill of responding is so powerful, you will want to be careful about giving advice or getting involved. A lot of times, a person will hold back until he or she sees how you react. If our response is one where you *tell* a person what to do, they may quit opening up or tell you only what they think *you* want to hear. At the highest level of responding, you are actually giving the reason for the feeling. In this way, you make the person's feeling clearer and more understandable.

> **RESPONDING** at the highest level reflects meaning:
> You feel _____ because _____.

It is also important to capture whether the person is seeing him- or herself as responsible or seeing someone else as being responsible. In the beginning of the exchange, your response should reflect where he or she sees the responsibility, even though you may not agree. By doing this, you will have a better chance of getting the person to open up. You can always disagree when it becomes necessary and effective to do so. Remember, if you have this skill, you can choose to use it. If you *don't* have this skill, you do not have the choice to use it at all.

DVD **RAPPORT BUILDING: Responding to Meaning — The *Wrong* Way and the *Right* Way**

Practice

Consider this scenario when providing answers below:

> Your partner has just come home from work. He/she looks "down" emotionally. You ask, "How was your day?" and your partner responds, "I don't know if I can take my new boss's constant micro-managing. I think he's trying to run me off."

Identify the intensity and category of your partner's feeling, and pick an accurate "feeling" word to describe the person's emotion.

Feeling Word: _____

Now supply the reason for your partner's feeling. What does the situation really mean to him or her? Who is your partner blaming? Why is all of this so important to your partner? What does this mean to your partner? Put yourself in your partner's place. Recognize the meaning, and then write a response.

Respond to Feeling and Meaning:

You feel _____ because _____

_____

_____

Action Strategies

Below are some Responding Strategies you may want to use in your personal relationships if the situation allows for it.

1. The next time your partner looks as if something is wrong and the situation allows for it, *nonverbally attend* and *mentally attend* to him or her. As your partner begins to talk, *respond to the content* of his or her statements three times, utilizing either of the following sentence formats to begin your response to the content:

    "You're saying _____(content)_____ ."

    "You're telling me _____(content)_____ ."

    "What I'm hearing is _____(content)_____ ."

2. The next time you perceive that your partner is having a difficult time emotionally based on how they look (i.e., what your observation skills tell you), respond to their feelings.

    For example, your partner comes home from work and appears fatigued. You say:

    "You look *worn out*."
    "You look *stressed*."
    "You look *tired*."
    "You look ___(try another feeling word here)___ ."

3. You notice your partner is becoming angry with you during a difference of opinion. Try using your *responding to feeling and meaning* skills before the situation escalates.

For example, your partner is not happy with your work schedule and starts to tell you about it. When your partner finishes telling you about his/her situation, use the following possible sentence formats and respond to his/her feelings and meaning:

"You're *mad* because of *my new work schedule*."

"You're feeling *aggravated* because *the new work schedule is taking time away from us*."

"You're feeling ___(your feeling word)___ because ___(the meaning you would use)___."

4. Once you have become proficient at utilizing responding to content, responding to feeling, and responding to feeling and meaning, try to combine the use of them in other situations where your partner is emotional about something going on in their life.

Note: Keep in mind that responding skills may not feel comfortable to you if you have not used them before. This is especially true if you have a tendency to want to give advice or take control of a situation too quickly.

Now, write a Responding Action Strategy:

_____

_____

_____

_____

_____

Rapport Building: Asking Relevant Questions

Asking Relevant Questions is something we all do. Unfortunately, the *way* we ask questions can actually break down rapport—especially if it is done incorrectly or like an interrogation. We will focus on asking questions that build rapport between you and your partner.

You ask questions in order to get useful answers. Some questions get better answers than others. The skill of asking relevant questions will help you increase your information base and, hence, your ability to help your partner.

There are really two basic steps involved in asking relevant questions in an effective way. Having responded to a person (discussed in the previous section) at the most accurate level, you must develop one or more **questions of the 5WH type**: Who, What, Where, When, Why, and How. Second, you must respond to the answer or answers given by the person to make sure you fully understand all the implications. Did you get the information you wanted? Was new information revealed?

How to Be in a Personal Relationship

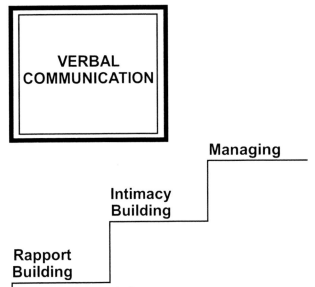

VERBAL COMMUNICATION

Managing

Intimacy Building

Rapport Building

1. *Responding techniques*
   - *Content*
     - *Reflect on what was seen and heard*
     - *Use a responding format to respond to content*
   - *Feeling*
     - *Reflect on feeling*
     - *Reflect on feeling and intensity*
   - *Meaning*
     - *Reflect on feeling and reason for that feeling*
     - *Respond to the feeling and meaning*
2. *Asking relevant questions*
   - *Using the 5WH method*
   - *Reflecting on answers and recycling*

Asking relevant questions will help you relate to your partner. The more you know about what is happening to your partner, the better able you understand his or her needs. Many people do not answer questions fully or accurately. In fact, questions will sometimes have the opposite effect. That is, they will shut off communication with people rather than open it up. This is because questions are often seen as the "bullets of the enemy" ("Cover up, here they come!"). The only way questions can really be effective in getting a person to open up is when they are used *in addition to* the nonverbal attending skills plus responding. Use of the previous skills can get a person to the point where they will talk quite openly without asking questions. It is then that questions can make their contribution by getting to some of the necessary specifics (Who, What, When, Where, Why, and How—the 5WH system) that your responding skills did not.

Kate and Russell have been dating for about six months. Recently, while having lunch downtown, Russell saw Kate coming out of a restaurant talking to a man. Kate kissed the man on the cheek as she walked away.

Kate and Russell had a dinner date scheduled for that night. All day, Russell kept thinking about Kate kissing the man on the cheek. He decided that he would discuss it with her during dinner.

As Kate and Russell were seated for dinner, Russell decided to ask Kate about her day. Below is how their dialogue went from this point on:

Russell: How was lunch today?

Kate: It was fine.

Russell: Why did you go out for lunch today?

Kate: I go out to lunch a couple of times per week.

Russell: What did you have for lunch?

Kate: Soup.

Russell: Do you make a habit of going to lunch at that restaurant?

Kate: What?

Russell: Do you make it a habit of going to that restaurant?

Kate: What are you talking about?

Russell: Do you make it a habit of keeping secrets?

Kate: I don't like your tone.

Russell: Do you always get angry when you are lying?

Kate: Lying about what?

Russell: How long have you been stepping out on me?

Kate: What are you talking about? I think we need to start this conversation over again.

Russell: Where do you get off sneaking around on me?

Kate: I think I need to leave. I have no idea what you are talking about. I feel like I am being interrogated, and I don't appreciate it.

(continued)

Russell:	I saw you today with that guy at lunch. The one you were kissing.
Kate:	You saw me at lunch. Kissing a guy. (Pauses for a second) All right. I get it. I was downtown having lunch, and I ran into my stepbrother, Ronnie. My parents were divorced 20 years ago. My father remarried and had Ronnie 18 years ago. He is a freshman at a local college. He called me at work today to talk about my dad. He's worried about Dad's health. I never mentioned Ronnie because we never talked about my parents being divorced. I didn't bring up my parent's divorce because you told me when we started dating that you didn't believe in divorce and felt people who divorced were weak.
	(Stands up) You got any more questions before I call a cab? This dinner is over.

Using the 5WH Method. Answers to questions will give you the detail you need to understand people or situations. The more details you know, the better you can understand what is going on. You always want to know **who** is involved, **what** they are doing or are going to do, **when** and **where** something happened or will happen, **how** it's going to be done or how it was done, and **why** an event is taking place.

"Where were you?"
"Who were you with?"
"Why were you there?"
"What did you actually do?"
"When did all this happen?"
"How was it handled?"

Obviously, Russell should have asked a more relevant question such as

"I saw you downtown today around lunchtime. I noticed you kissing a young man on the cheek as you left Joe's Café. I felt a little heart tug. Is everything okay with us?"

When you have all this information, you can take appropriate action and/or prevent problems from happening—not only now but maybe in the future. Question-asking can be used with responding or when you simply choose to assist with a problem.

If Russell had used this approach and responded by telling Kate, "I saw (observed) you today kissing a guy on the cheek, etc.," before he asked his series of questions as an interrogation, he would have prevented a lot of problems.

Responding opens up the person and gives you a chance to make sure you understand what is going on. It also builds up trust with a person. For these reasons, you should always try to respond to a partner's actions or words at the highest possible level before you actually start asking questions. The answers to your questions will fill in the details of the picture. Often, details, or reasons, come from responding skills alone—if you have patience. If they do not, questions are appropriate. It's as simple as that.

ASKING RELEVANT QUESTIONS means
using the 5WH method (Who, What, When, Where, Why, and How) to get as much detail as possible.

Practice

For each of the following situations, first make a response, and then ask a relevant question.

1. Your partner has been late three times in the past two weeks, but has not called in to let you know. Your partner says, "Look, I know this looks bad. I'm sorry, but I'd rather not talk about why I have been late."

    Respond: "You feel _____ because _____

    _____ ."

    Question (5WH): _____

    _____ ?

2. Your partner says the following to you: "I don't think it's fair that we always go to your family for the holidays. It doesn't make any sense. It's not right!"

    Respond: "You feel _____ because _____

    _____ ."

    Question (5WH): _____

    _____ ?

Reflecting on answers and recycling. It's not enough just to ask good questions. You also have to be able to make sense out of the answers you get—and recognize as well what answers you're still not getting. Begin by responding to the answer: "You're saying _____" or "So you feel _____." Then *reflect* on (i.e., observe and listen) or think carefully about the answer to your question.

Your partner may be leveling with you and giving you the information you need to help. And even though he or she may be doing the best he/she can to provide you with all the information you need, they may inadvertently be leaving out some vital details. Or your partner may be covering up something. In that case, your partner is still not fully communicating with you. Your observation skills are critical here. How do they look? What are they doing? What did they say? What *didn't* they say?

ASKING RELEVANT QUESTIONS means reflecting
on answers and thinking about what you have—
and have not—learned.

When reflecting on your partner's answers to your questions, you can think about four specific things:

- How your partner looks as he/she answers (relaxed, uncomfortable)
- What your partner is doing while he/she answers (facing and making eye contact, looking away, looking down at his/her feet)
- What your partner actually said (the information content of the answer)
- What your partner may have failed to say (any "gaps" in the way he/she answers)

By reflecting on these four areas of concern, you can make sure that you fully understand all the implications of the answer. Once you've responded to this answer, you can ask additional questions to get the rest of the information you need. By using your nonverbal and mental attending, responding, asking good questions, reflecting, and then responding again—you'll be recycling.

ASKING RELEVANT QUESTIONS means recycling
by asking good questions, reflecting on the
answers, and then responding again.

Let's go back to Kate and Russell's situation where Russell sees Kate downtown around lunchtime kissing a young man on the cheek as she was leaving a restaurant. We now know it was her stepbrother, but let's look at how Russell could have used the skills discussed above and had a better outcome.

Making the Point—The RIGHT Way
The Case of Russell's Rewind

Kate and Russell are now in the restaurant for dinner, and Russell begins to inquire about seeing Kate downtown at lunchtime.

Russell: Kate, I saw you downtown today, around lunchtime. I was out to lunch with Jim Dane. Anyway, I noticed you coming out of Jose's Café with a young guy, and I saw you kiss him on the cheek. *(responding to content: "I saw you" using observation skills)*

Kate: (Uneasy based on her facial expression.) That was my stepbrother, Ronnie. He's 20 and goes to college in the area. He called me this morning about our father.

Russell: You have a stepbrother, Ronnie? You looked uneasy when you said that. Why didn't you tell me you had a stepbrother? *(recycle, respond to feeling and meaning, ask another relevant question)*

Kate: I was uneasy because my parents divorced, and you mentioned that you didn't respect people who get divorced.

Russell: You felt anxious about telling me about your parents being divorced because I told you I'm against divorce. When did I say that? *(recycle, respond to feeling and meaning, ask another relevant question)*

Kate: About five weeks ago when you and I were going to meet my dad and mom, well stepmom, and I cancelled it at the last minute. That's why I cancelled it.

Russell: You're telling me you cancelled dinner with your parents because of what I said about divorce? I'm sorry you took it that way. When were you going to tell me? *(recycle, respond to feeling and meaning, ask another relevant question)*

Kate: I don't know, but I respect your stance on divorce, and this relationship means a lot to me.

How to Be in a Personal Relationship

In this scenario, because Russell asked questions skillfully, he not only resolved his concern about Kate kissing the young man (her step-brother), but he also found out how important his values were to Kate and how important the relationship she has with him is.

DVD

> **RAPPORT BUILDING: Asking Relevant Questions**
> **— The *Wrong* Way and the *Right* Way**

Action Strategies

Below are some Strategies for Asking Relevant Questions you may want to use in your personal relationships if the situation allows for it.

1. The next time you "observe" your partner looking tired or stressed when they come in the door, **respond to how they look:** "You look worn out." Then **ask a relevant 5WH question** such as, "How was your day?" Then **recycle their answer** by responding to their answer: "You're telling me that ___(content of statement)___."

2. The next time you hear your partner sounding anxious based on their tone of voice, **respond to how they sound:** "You sound uneasy." Then **ask a relevant question** such as: "What happened that made you uneasy?" Then **recycle their answer** to your question: "You're saying _____ caused you to be uneasy."

3. While having dinner with your partner (if the situation allows for it), try using the **asking questions skills** discussed above. Keep in mind to try to nonverbally and mentally attend while applying the skills. Also, remember that just responding can facilitate your partner opening up without asking any questions.

Now, write an Asking Relevant Questions Action Strategy:

_____

_____

_____

_____

_____

Intimacy Building

A key to personal relationship success is the ability to maintain intimacy. Intimacy means to become close to, or more personal with, another person.

Many couples in personal relationships misconstrue passion for intimacy. There is no doubt that passion can be a catalyst for intimacy, but they are not the same.

Passion is the emotional intensity component of a relationship. To be passionate is the degree of emotion one attaches to something or someone. Passion is like the emotional thermostat of a relationship. The higher the temperature, the more emotionally fused to the other person you are. The lower the temperature, the lower the emotional attachment is.

Intimacy is the degree to which we truly know another person. It is how well we know them physically, mentally, emotionally, and socially. By sleeping with another person and having a sexual relationship, we begin to know them physically. But knowing a person physically doesn't necessarily tell us how that person truly thinks, feels, and relates to others in the world. When another person wants to appear attractive to us, they are not likely to reveal aspects of themselves that might make them appear unattractive. They will put their proverbial "best foot forward." The concept of "getting to know someone" has always been a positive principle to consider before letting them get close to you.

It is also important to keep in mind that all of us have flaws. We are not perfect creatures. We bring histories with us to every new relationship, and these histories are not always positive. Consequently, to love someone requires a willingness to understand another person's imperfections. The question for all of us to consider is, "Am I willing to accommodate and tolerate this other person's imperfections?" The answer to this question is often a matter of personal values.

Of course, we can't forget that humans are capable of change. If they bring with them patterns of behavior based on history, many of those patterns can be modified through new learning experiences.

Making the Point—The RIGHT Way
The Case of the Beauty that was More than Skin Deep

Tricia was a very attractive young woman. She had a rule for herself that if she was going to be with a man, he had to meet a certain standard for physical attractiveness.

Three years ago, she met a man named Randy at a friend's house. Randy was a very nice guy. Every time she encountered Randy, he was constantly attentive and non-intrusive, with a great sense of humor. Randy had started his own business when he was 22. He was 30 when Tricia met him.

From a physical standpoint, Randy was not attractive to Tricia. Randy's hygiene was good, but his grooming needed improvement. He was also somewhat overweight. Randy didn't like to exercise.

Tricia and Randy developed a very close friendship, talking several times a week on the phone. As Tricia got to know Randy, she came to realize that Randy had grown up poor. His father left his mother when Randy was 12 years old, and he had two younger brothers. Randy had related to Tricia that he became the father figure for his two younger brothers. He had gotten his first job at 13 years old, working at a neighborhood restaurant.

Randy told Tricia he had given everything he earned from every job he held until he was 17 to his mother to help her financially. He told Tricia his two brothers eventually went to college, and he had helped pay their tuition through his business.

As time went on, Tricia began to notice a change in Randy. He had begun to lose weight, and he was dressing differently. His hairstyle had changed, too. Tricia had also noticed that his smile had changed. When she first met him, he would sometimes put his hand over his mouth when talking. Now, he had a warm, open smile that he seemed proud to show. The changes in Randy were so subtle that Tricia didn't notice them as they were occurring.

One day, while with a college friend, she met Randy for lunch. Following the lunch, Tricia's friend commented on what a great guy Randy was and how cute he was. The friend then stated that she couldn't understand why Tricia wasn't more interested in Randy—especially since he was so obviously interested in Tricia.

Tricia left the lunch thinking she must be clueless about Randy. She called Randy that night. She asked Randy how he felt about her, something she had never even considered. Randy hesitated. Then he said he had wished that someday they could be more than friends, but he had come to realize that Tricia wasn't interested in him that way.

(continued)

(concluded)

As their conversation continued, she asked Randy about the changes in his appearance. Randy was surprised—he didn't think she had noticed. So Randy told Tricia how he had decided about a year ago that if he was going to be more than friends with her, he had to work on himself physically. He had gotten a personal trainer to improve his body image, a dentist to improve the appearance of his teeth, and a hair stylist to update his look. Randy quietly confided that he had always been aware that his physical appearance needed improvement. He had just needed the motivation to do it—and Tricia was that motivation.

Tricia and Randy were married a year later.

In the story you just read, Tricia had developed an intimate relationship with Randy, but not a passionate or physical one. By becoming friends with Randy, she got to know him as a person. She learned things about him she may not have learned if they hadn't started out as friends. She found out that beneath the surface, Randy was a terrific person. She also realized that beauty is more than skin deep.

Randy realized after meeting Tricia that his physical appearance was important if he was going to have Tricia in his life. He had always known he was neglectful of his physical appearance, and his relationship with Tricia gave him the reinforcement he needed to modify his behaviors and, consequently, his appearance.

Intimacy is the ability to get to know someone better than anyone else knows them. It is critical to establishing and maintaining a relationship over time.

We will discuss two intimacy building skills: self-disclosure skills and reinforcing skills.

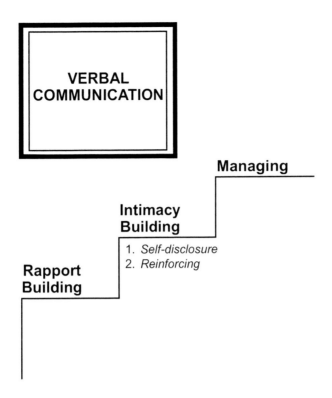

Intimacy Building: Self-Disclosure Skills

Self-disclosure is the ability to express personal facts, thoughts, and feelings about yourself to a partner in a personal relationship. It is also the ability to facilitate your partner's willingness to self-disclose with you.

The purpose of self-disclosure is to increase intimacy between two people. It does this by providing an openness about who we are to another person and facilitates a willingness for the other person to reciprocate. A secondary purpose is to promote trust by removing barriers to knowing who we are. When others know us well, they not only trust us more, they understand our needs and can fulfill them more easily.

There are benefits to self-disclosure. When we feel someone knows us well and still accepts us, we are less anxious being around them. We do not have to be "on guard" as much.

A second benefit of self-disclosure is related to loneliness. When we believe people truly know us and accept us, we don't feel alone in the world. We know they are there for us despite who we are or what our needs are. They accept us for better, and more importantly, for worse. This is often referred to as unconditional love.

There are four skills involved in Self-disclosure: Knowing the guidelines, Knowing the types of disclosures, Expressing disclosures, and Receiving disclosures.

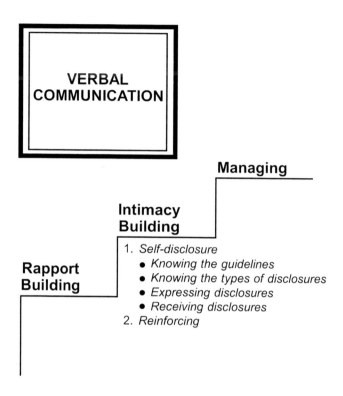

Knowing the Guidelines. There are some guidelines to consider before self-disclosing. These guidelines are important to implement because self-disclosures that do not follow them can cause personal relationship problems.

The first guideline is to *not* have a disclosure about yourself that is not true. In other words, do not misrepresent who you are to a potential partner. All too often, we tend to exaggerate who we are or what we have accomplished in order to impress another. Conversely, we may downplay negative things about ourselves for the same reason.

The second guideline is to pay attention to the depth and timing of a disclosure. Telling someone very personal information about yourself too soon into a relationship may make them uneasy. A good rule of thumb is to keep the level of disclosures to another person close to their levels of disclosures to you. For example, telling someone when you first meet them that you had a problem with drug abuse is probably not a good idea until they have seen and heard a lot of your positive qualities.

How to Be in a Personal Relationship

A third guideline is to pay attention to the duration and amount of information you disclose about yourself. Someone who is always talking about themselves and never letting their partner talk is not fun to be with. A good rule of thumb is to keep the duration and amount of time you disclose in balance with your partner's disclosure amount.

A fourth guideline is to never reveal to another person a personal self-disclosure your partner has revealed to you. This is especially true if it is a negative or embarrassing one. It would be analogous to a form of infidelity or unfaithfulness.

> **SELF-DISCLOSURE** means the appropriate sharing of personal information that is factual, not exaggerated, in keeping with the other person's level of sharing, and timely.

Making the Point—The RIGHT Way
The Case of "Getting to Know You"

Wanda and Jerome have been dating for two months. They really enjoy each other's company. Jerome tends to be quiet but a good listener. Wanda wishes she knew more about Jerome. She knows what Jerome does for a living, where he attended college, where he lives, etc., but Jerome has never mentioned his family. Wanda feels she would like to know about Jerome's family and decides that she would like to approach him when they have dinner at her apartment.

They have just finished dinner and Wanda initiates the following conversation.

Wanda: Jerome, I really enjoy our time together. I was wondering why you have never discussed your family. *(appropriate depth and timing)*

Jerome: (Hesitantly) It's not something I like to talk about.

Wanda: That's okay, I'll let it go.

Jerome: You have a right to know.

Wanda: I don't want to pry.

Jerome: It's okay. I don't like to talk about it, but I never knew my father. He left when I was 2 years old. *(appropriate depth)*

Wanda: I'm sorry.

Jerome: I have two brothers and a sister. (Jerome then became silent.)

(continued)

(concluded)

Wanda:	You don't have to talk about it. (After a brief silence) I never told you about my mom, but she was diagnosed with a mental illness when I was 10. It was hard on my dad and us. She eventually got well on medication. *(appropriate depth and timing)*
Jerome:	Well, my mom did the best she could, but the pressure got to her and she began using drugs. I was six when I was put in foster care. *(appropriate duration and amount)*
Wanda:	What happened to your brothers and sister?
Jerome:	We were all split up in different foster care homes. I haven't seen my older brother since I was eight. I saw my sister two years ago. My younger brother died in a car accident. *(duration and amount)*
Wanda:	I'm sorry. You don't have to say any more.
Jerome:	It's okay. You have a neat family and I was embarrassed about mine.
Wanda:	My family is not perfect. My older brother was involved in drugs and he still has problems. *(appropriate depth and timing)* (After a brief silence) This is your personal business. You tell my family what you want to tell them, when you want to tell them. *(confidentiality)*

Knowing the Types of Disclosures. Self-disclosures take many forms. There are disclosures of personal **facts** such as how old you are, where you live or went to school, and who your parents are. Disclosures can also be facts about personal life experiences you've had.

There are disclosures of personal **thoughts**. This would include personal beliefs such as religious/moral beliefs. It could also include your thoughts about other people or your thoughts on a particular subject (e.g., a political opinion). Just be aware, if the other person thinks differently from you, it can cause conflict.

There are disclosures about personal **feelings**. For example, telling your partner how you really feel about another person, or about them, or about a personal issue are examples of feeling disclosures. For instance, telling your partner that you do not like a friend of his/hers, or you don't share the same food likes/dislikes may invalidate your partner's feelings. Keep in mind that telling someone you don't feel the way they do can be threatening and cause conflicts.

There are disclosures about personal **needs**. A personal need is tell-ing someone you want them to do something for you that involves an action. For example, you and your partner are visiting a friend's house when you partner says "I don't feel well. Could we leave and go home? I feel nauseous." Or, what if your partner says, "I know you're not aware of this, but when you make jokes about my family, I get tired of it. I need you to stop doing that. I know they are not perfect, but they are my family!"

Self-disclosures describing yourself can be **positive** or **negative**. Although we like to put our "best foot forward" and reveal disclosures that make us look positive, we don't want to come across as bragging. For example, if you have a tendency to tell someone about all your suc-cesses and strengths, it could be a real turnoff. On the other hand, if you are always disclosing negative aspects of yourself, you may give the impression that you have no confidence. A good rule of thumb is to bal-ance the negative and positive self-disclosures with a partner. It makes you appear human.

> **SELF-DISCLOSURE** means knowing the types of self-disclosures (facts, thoughts, feelings, and needs) and when to use them.

Practice

Write down two factual self-disclosures you have never told your partner.

Example: I had an eating disorder when I was a teenager.

1. _____
2. _____

Write down two thoughts (ideas, dreams) you have had that you never disclosed to your partner.

Example: I always wanted to go to college.

1. _____
2. _____

Write down two feelings you've had toward a partner that you have trouble disclosing.

Example: I get angry when you put down my family.

1. _____

2. _____

Write down two positive self-disclosures about yourself.

Example: I won a beauty pageant in high school.

1. _____

2. _____

Write down two negative self-disclosures about yourself.

Example: I flunked out of college my freshman year.

1. _____

2. _____

Making the Point—The WRONG Way
The Case of the Forthright Fool

Renee and Scott have just started dating. They are on their third date at a nice restaurant. The date is going well until the following dialogue takes place.

Renee: What's your favorite TV show?

Scott: I don't like TV. Most of the shows are juvenile. I like to read instead. *(inappropriate thinking and feeling self-disclosure)*

Renee: Well I don't think all TV shows are juvenile.

Scott: I think that people who watch TV are letting their brains go to mush. *(inappropriate thinking self-disclosure)*

Renee: I'm sorry you don't like television. There are some shows that are educational, such as those on the Discovery Channel or The Learning Channel.

Scott: I would like to change the subject. I hope you don't mind. *(inappropriate thinking self-disclosure)*

(continued)

How to Be in a Personal Relationship

Renee:	No, I don't mind.
Scott:	How far did you go in school?
Renee:	I wanted to go to college, but I had to quit my freshman year and go back to work.
Scott:	I wanted to quit myself, but I hung in there and did well. It was tough, but worth it. *(inappropriate positive self-disclosure)*
Renee:	(Beginning to get annoyed) What are you saying? Are you implying that I may have been weak because I quit?
Scott:	(Somewhat embarrassed) I'm sorry you took it that way. I was just letting you know how I experienced college.
Renee:	Okay.
Scott:	I just believe in being forthright with people. I guess you're not comfortable with that. *(inappropriate thinking self-disclosure)*
Renee:	(Angry) I want to be forthright with you. You are an arrogant, pseudo intellectual bore. How do you like my forthrightness? *(appropriate thinking self-disclosure)*
	Renee calls the waiter over and says, "Could you call me a cab?" *(appropriate need)*

Expressing Disclosures. When you have decided you want to reveal something to a partner, there are several factors to consider. Knowing the guidelines for disclosing and the different types of disclosures is critical.

It is also important to apply your nonverbal attending skills when communicating your disclosures. The use of nonverbal attending tells your partner that what you are about to disclose is important. Your mental attending skills (visual and listening) should also be utilized to determine whether it is a good time to make a self-disclosure. If your mental attending skills tell you your partner is tired, angry, distracted, etc., it may not be a good time to communicate a negative self-disclosure. On the other hand, a positive self disclosure such as, "I hope you know how much I love and respect you," may be a good self-disclosure to make to a tired, angry partner.

If the expressing of a self-disclosure is not received well by your partner, you may want to utilize your rapport-building skills to get back on track. For example, your partner becomes angry at you when you admit (disclose) that you may have bounced some checks. You may want to consider using your responding skills if he/she becomes angry to de-escalate the tension and return to a meaningful conversation that includes disclosures.

> **EXPRESSING DISCLOSURES** means utilizing your nonverbal and mental attending skills, as well as your rapport-building skills, to determine the timing and types of disclosure you should make.

Receiving Disclosures. The receiving of a partner's disclosures requires the nonverbal attending skills, mental attending skills, and rapport-building skills discussed previously. These are important because these skills can motivate a partner to want to disclose. If a partner realizes you are not nonverbally attending to his/her disclosure, your partner may discontinue disclosing. If you don't apply your mental attending skills of looking and listening, you may miss or misinterpret important aspects of your partner's disclosure. If you don't utilize your rapport-building skills of responding and asking relevant questions, your partner may feel judged. This may result in their not sharing their true thoughts, feelings, and needs in the future.

> **RECEIVING DISCLOSURES** means using your nonverbal and mental attending skills, as well as your rapport-building skills, to encourage your partner's sharing of personal thoughts, feelings, and needs.

Making the Point—The RIGHT Way
The Case of Disclosures Done Well

Lola and Jared have been married for three years. Lola loves Jared, but has become concerned about his family's treatment of her. Lola feels that Jared's parents think that Jared should not have married her. She thinks that Jared's parents don't like the fact that she is of Mexican descent.

Lola and Jared are talking about having children, and Lola noticed that Jared's mother is putting pressure on Jared to wait. Lola thinks it's because Jared's mother is hoping their relationship ends before they have children. She is hurt, angry, and confused as to why Jared doesn't seem to notice it. Lola decides she wants to disclose to Jared her thoughts, feelings and needs, and she decides she will have this discussion on Sunday afternoon after church.

When Lola and Jared arrive home from church, Lola asks, "Can we go into the den and talk about something?" To which Jared responds, "Sure, you look anxious." *(rapport-building skill: responding to feeling)*

(Jared and Lola are now sitting on the couch across from each other.)

Lola:	This is hard for me to say, but I've got to say it. *(emotion self-disclosure)*
Jared:	Go ahead, I'm listening. *(nonverbal and mentally attending)*
Lola:	I don't think your mother has accepted me as your wife. *(thinking self-disclosure)*
Jared:	Okay.
Lola:	I think she really never wanted us to get married because of my Hispanic heritage. *(thinking self-disclosure)*
Jared:	I think you are probably right, but I don't care what she thinks. *(thinking and emotional self-disclosure)*
Lola:	You mean you know?
Jared:	I've talked with my mother about it several times because I know you can sense it, and it has to hurt. *(rapport-building skill: responding)*
Lola:	Why haven't you said anything? *(relevant question)*
Jared:	I was afraid it would cause problems between you and me. *(emotional self-disclosure)*
	My dad thinks the world of you. He and Mom have had disagreements about her attitude toward you. *(factual self-disclosure)*

(continued)

(concluded)

Lola:	Your dad does think the world of me! *(factual self-disclosure)*
Jared:	Yes, but you know Dad, he's one of those quiet types and doesn't like to show his emotions. He really respects you and the patience you have shown toward my mother's attitude. *(factual self-disclosure)*
Lola:	I didn't know.
Jared:	Lola, I love you dearly. I respect you for your poise, patience, and willingness to put up with Mother's prejudice attitude. *(emotional self-disclosure)*
	I also want you and I to start having children. It's about time. I told my dad. He was excited about being a grandfather. Don't worry about Mom, I'll deal with it. She'll change. *(factual and thinking self-disclosure)*

DVD

INTIMACY BUILDING: Self-Disclosure
— The *Wrong* Way and the *Right* Way

Action Strategies

Below are some Self-Disclosure Strategies you may want to use in your personal relationships if the situation allows for it.

1. Make a factual self-disclosure to your partner about an experience in your life that had an emotional impact on you.

2. Ask your partner to tell you about something they have always dreamed about doing.

   - Nonverbally and mentally attend while they tell you.
   - Respond to their disclosure and ask relevant questions to facilitate their talking about it.

3. Tell your partner something about yourself that you would like to improve on with regard to your relationship with them.

   Example: "I'm not a good listener when you and I talk, and I want to improve."

4. The next time you observe your partner doing something that you respect, self-disclose your thoughts and feelings about it.

   Example: "I love to watch you being a mother to our children—you're so good at it."

5. Ask your partner to self-disclose something they feel and think about you that they would like to change.

   Example: They tell you that they wish you would compliment the things they do right more often.

Now, write a Self-Disclosure Action Strategy:

_____

_____

_____

_____

_____

Intimacy Building: Reinforcing/Nonreinforcing

We reinforce desirable behaviors that we want to reoccur or occur more often, and we nonreinforce, or punish, undesirable behaviors that we want to occur less often, or maybe not at all. Reinforcing and nonreinforcing behaviors may be either verbal or nonverbal.

The four steps of Reinforcing/Nonreinforcing Behavior are Reinforcing Verbally, Reinforcing Nonverbally, Nonreinforcing Verbally, and Nonreinforcing Nonverbally.

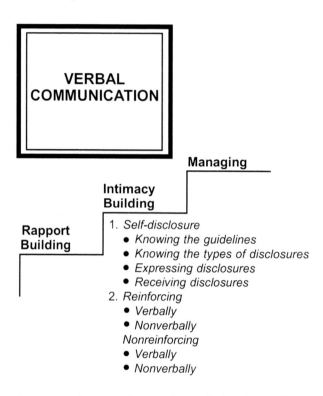

Reinforcing. In general, people perform behaviors that give them a good feeling, and they avoid behaviors that make them feel uncomfortable. The problem is that we often experience those good feelings (i.e., feel rewarded) for behaviors that are undesirable or inappropriate. For example, criminals who go uncaught are reinforced by the attention and material gain. Parents often reinforce complaining children in grocery stores by giving them sweets. Some managers receive the adulation of their peers for their use of force. In these examples, the rewards that accompany the criminal behavior, the public complaining, and the use of force almost certainly guarantee that these behaviors will continue and may even increase in frequency.

How to Be in a Personal Relationship

Maya and Esteban have been married for two years and have no children. Maya constantly tries to please Esteban by doing extra things for him like cooking special meals and organizing his clothes, but Esteban rarely comments, and if he does comment, it's usually negative. Maya has grown weary of Esteban's lack of appreciation and has decided they need some space. It is Friday evening, and Esteban has criticized Maya about the dinner she has prepared. Below is a typical dialogue.

Esteban: (Displaying a negative facial expression and angry tone) Can't you even prepare a meal right? (The meal is fine—he's just in a bad mood.)

Maya: (Showing concern on her face with anxious tone of voice) What's wrong with it?

Esteban: (Rolling his eyes with a sarcastic tone) More like what's right with it?

Maya: (Angry facial expression and tone of voice) That's it! I've had it. You never have anything positive to say to me. You've always got that same negative look on your face and that whiny tone of voice when you don't get your way. I'm sorry, but I'm not your mother.

Esteban: (Stunned facial expression) What's got you so wound up? I was just commenting on the meal.

Maya: (Angry expression on her face with assertive tone of voice) I think we need some space. I can't stand living with somebody who never shows any positive appreciation for the things that somebody else does for them.

Maya then grabs her car keys and leaves the house.

Reinforcement refers to the use of rewards to maintain or increase desired behaviors. Reinforcement can be given by both verbal and nonverbal feedback to partners.

> **REINFORCING** means using verbal and/or nonverbal responses as ways to maintain and/or increase desired behaviors.

Reinforcing Verbally. Verbal reinforcement means saying something with the intention of maintaining or increasing a desired behavior. Most of the time, the words we choose are experienced as pleasant by the person we're talking to. We've all heard or said these phrases: "Bob, thank you for always being there," or "Sarah, I appreciate you taking the responsibility for that without being asked," or "I love you."

Unfortunately, we are probably also familiar with words or phrases that are *not* experienced as pleasant, but are still aimed at maintaining or increasing a desired behavior. For example, when one woman asked her husband how he liked dinner, he replied, "Of course I liked it. What are you looking for, a compliment? That's your job."

In personal relationships, an understanding of reinforcing skills is critical to maintaining intimacy between you and a partner. Conversely, lack of reinforcing skills can lead to a decrease in intimacy between you and a partner.

Of course, a key in any personal relationship is knowing how to reinforce a partner's behaviors that are desirable to you and the relationship and *not* reinforce behaviors that are undesirable to you or the relationship.

Which response would you prefer? "Great dinner. Thanks!" or "That's your job!"

DVD

REINFORCING: Verbally
— The *Wrong* Way and the *Right* Way

Reinforcing Nonverbally. Nonverbal reinforcement means using nonverbal cues to maintain or increase desired behaviors. The most obvious nonverbal cues are smiling, giving a kiss, nodding the head, and giving a pat on the back. For example, your partner has just set out your clothes for work. You look directly at them and smile. The smile will probably be experienced as pleasant and may lead your partner to repeat the behavior.

Some nonverbal cues might be intended to reinforce a behavior, but actually might be experienced as less than pleasant. For example, Jim is having difficulty with a computer task. He calls out to his partner for assistance. She says, "Sure," and walks over to where he is sitting, showing a willingness to help. When she arrives, she quickly sees what Jim is doing wrong. As he attempts to press the wrong computer key again, she grabs his hand and jerks it away from the keyboard, giving him a critical facial expression that implies he's stupid. Then she shows him the correct keys to press.

Her intent may have been to reinforce her willingness to help and educate Jim regarding the correct keys to press to accomplish the goal, but the way she conducted herself may have left Jim with an unpleasant feeling. If you were Jim what would you think?

DVD

> ### REINFORCING: Nonverbally
> ### — The *Wrong* Way and the *Right* Way

Nonreinforcing. Nonreinforcing, sometimes called punishment, means saying or doing something that is intended to reduce or eliminate an undesirable behavior. Again, this can be done using verbal and/or nonverbal feedback with your partner.

Although it is generally accepted that nonreinforcing is a tool of "last resort" for the skilled partner, its use is also determined by other factors such as the nature of the behavior, the context in which the behavior occurred, previous displays of the behavior, and the social rules (or etiquette) that apply to the behavior, among other factors. When administered fairly and appropriately, it can be a powerful way to change behaviors.

> **NONREINFORCING** means using verbal and/or nonverbal responses as ways to decrease or eliminate undesirable behaviors.

Nonreinforcing Verbally. Verbal nonreinforcement means saying something with the intention of decreasing or eliminating an undesirable behavior. These can be some of your most difficult conversations; therefore, your ability to size up the situation and use the skills previously discussed in this book will be invaluable here. And again, being polite can be your best approach. Examples of verbal nonreinforcement can be mild, such as, "Please do not do that behavior again," or intense, "Stop it NOW!" They can express feelings, such as, "I'm disappointed that you chose to behave that way," or they can be explanatory, "Let's talk about this behavior. You know, we've talked about this on two previous occasions, and now it's occurred again."

Insults and hurtful statements are also examples of verbal nonreinforcement. "I can't believe you're so stupid that you still haven't finished paying the bills. Grandma was slow, but she was old! Hurry up!" or "Only an idiot would try to do it that way."

Which of these verbal nonreinforcements would you prefer to receive—the mild statements or the hurtful ones?

Nonreinforcing Nonverbally. Nonverbal nonreinforcing means using nonverbal cues to decrease or eliminate undesired behaviors. The most obvious nonverbal cues are shaking your head back and forth indicating, "No" or "Stop," looking at your partner with a serious expression communicating displeasure, and rolling the eyes. Other nonverbal nonreinforcing involves withholding behaviors that you might normally do for your partner in an effort to reduce or eliminate an undesired behavior. For instance, after being criticized or insulted regarding the preparation of a meal, a partner may refuse to cook a meal for a while. Or a partner may withhold intimacy to encourage a change in a partner's behaviors.

Some less productive nonverbal nonreinforcing includes slapping, hitting, punching, pinching, and other physically abusive behaviors. The use of obscene and/or exaggerated gestures of disgust, contempt, and displeasure are also considered ineffective.

A Word of Caution: Nonreinforcing behaviors, or punishment, may not be a wise choice over the long term. Science has found that the use of these types of behaviors is most effective if you use them each time an undesirable behavior occurs—difficult even under controlled laboratory circumstances. It has also been determined that nonreinforcing behaviors are *most* effective when they are used in combination with reinforcing behaviors. Our primary goal in presenting information regarding nonreinforcing behaviors is to provide you with information so that you will know it when you see it and stimulate your thinking so that you can make wise choices when managing the behaviors of other people.

Making the Point—The RIGHT Way
The Case of the Meddling Mother-in-Law

Sandra and Warren have been together for six years. They would describe their relationship as really good. But these days, Warren is frustrated with Sandra's mother's constant criticism of the two of them living together without being married. Sandra's mother also tends to make comments that lead Warren to believe that she feels he is not good enough to be married to Sandra. Warren and Sandra have just eaten lunch, and they are on the back porch of their home sitting across from each other.

Sandra: (Compassionate look on her face and sympathetic tone of voice) *(nonverbal reinforcer)* I really appreciate your patience with Mom. Since Dad died, she is just lost. *(verbal reinforcer)*

(continued)

How to Be in a Personal Relationship

(concluded)

Warren:	(Smiles, looks down, shakes his head and speaks with an amused tone) *(nonverbal reinforcer)* I'm glad you appreciate my patience, but it's wearing thin. *(verbal reinforcer and verbal nonreinforcer)*
Sandra:	(Sympathetic smile and says in an assertive tone) *(nonverbal reinforcer)* I will talk to her about the way she talks to you when the time is right. I appreciate your patience. *(verbal reinforcer)*
Warren:	(Looking uncertain and with a weary tone) *(nonverbal non-reinforcer)* I know it isn't easy for you, either. She's lucky she has you for a daughter. I respect that about you. *(verbal reinforcer)* But I'm losing patience about this. It's got to stop. *(verbal nonreinforcer)* I hope you know I love you. *(verbal reinforcer)*

Practice

List some **Verbal Reinforcers** you could give as a partner and the behaviors that would warrant them. (Remember that written statements are also included in this category, such as a love note, a thinking-of-you card, a letter, or even a thank you card.)

Example: **Verbal Reinforcer:** That was great!
Behavior: Prepared my favorite meal.

1. Verbal Reinforcer: _____
   Behavior: _____

2. Verbal Reinforcer: _____
   Behavior: _____

3. Verbal Reinforcer: _____
   Behavior: _____

List some **Nonverbal Reinforcers** you can administer as a partner and the behaviors that would receive them.

Example: **Nonverbal Reinforcer:** Smile
Behavior: Handed me something I asked for.

1. Nonverbal Reinforcer: _____

   Behavior: _____

2. Nonverbal Reinforcer: _____

   Behavior: _____

3. Nonverbal Reinforcer: _____

   Behavior: _____

List some **Verbal Nonreinforcers** you can administer as a partner and the behaviors that would warrant them:

Example: **Verbal Nonreinforcer:** "Don't do that!"
Behavior: Inappropriate touch

1. Verbal Nonreinforcer: _____

   Behavior: _____

2. Verbal Nonreinforcer: _____

   Behavior: _____

3. Verbal Nonreinforcer: _____

   Behavior: _____

List some **Nonverbal Nonreinforcers** you can administer as a partner and the behaviors that would warrant them:

Example: **Nonverbal Nonreinforcer:** Frown on your face
Behavior: Partner said something hurtful about my family

1. Nonverbal Nonreinforcer: _____

   Behavior: _____

2. Nonverbal Nonreinforcer: _____

   Behavior: _____

3. Nonverbal Nonreinforcer: _____

   Behavior: _____

Action Strategies

Below are some Reinforcing/Nonreinforcing Strategies you may want to use in your personal relationships if the situation allows for it.

1. Your partner does something for you without being asked that is very helpful to you.

   Say, "Thank you for ___(what he/she did)___. I appreciate your doing things for me that I need done without my having to ask."

2. Your partner says something to you that is complimentary to you.

   Look at them and utilize two nonverbal reinforcers right after they do it. (Examples: smile, thumbs up, kiss, etc.)

3. Your partner says something that hurts your feelings—and they have done it more than once lately.

   Use a verbal nonreinforcer, such as: "I don't know if you are aware of it, but when you said ___(what they said that hurt you)___, it really hurt me."

4. Your partner does something to you that you dislike.

   If they are looking at you when they do it, utilize a nonverbal nonreinforcer such as shaking your head in disapproval or giving a facial expression of disapproval.

Now, write a Reinforcing/Nonreinforcing Action Strategy:

_____

_____

_____

_____

_____

Managing

All relationships involve managing your own requests and needs as well as the requests and needs of those people who share your personal life. We are not defining managing as a *controlling* skill as we would if we were talking about the workplace or parenting. However, we *are* defining managing in the context of a personal relationship as the actions necessary to be taken by two adults who need to handle the day-to-day expectations of each partner. There will be numerous occasions in a personal relationship where there is a division of labor on who does what. There will also be numerous situations where one partner has to ask the other partner to do something. The other partner must then respond as to whether they can or cannot grant the request.

For example, the simple request of asking your partner to drive you somewhere, pick something up at the store, or help them with a household chore can interfere with your partner's personal needs at that moment. Conversely, how a partner manages the other partner's request—especially if the response is, "No, I can't help you"—has ramifications for that relationship depending on how the request and the response are managed.

Making the Point—The WRONG Way
The Case of Dave's Downfall

Dave has a reputation for applying the rules when they suit him and always saying, "No," just because he feels like it. Dave has been married to his wife, June, for 20 years. Both of their children moved out of the house following high school. June has informed Dave that she wants a divorce now that the children are gone. She told Dave that their marriage, for the most part, had been a failure due to Dave's over-controlling nature and his know-it-all attitude toward her and the children. She pointed out that he was always neglecting her needs and the needs of his children. But when either she or one of the kids couldn't satisfy one of his requests or needs, he would become angry. Dave was shocked. He knew they had problems, but not to the point of divorce.

One evening, Dave was drinking at his favorite bar. He was feeling pretty down. June had just moved out, leaving him alone in the house. Knowing that he'd had too much to drink, he called three friends for a ride home. All three said they were busy, and they told him to take a cab. Then, he called June. June also turned down his request for help and told him to take a cab home.

(continued)

Dave became angry, and then decided to drive his vehicle home—despite having downed a few drinks.

About five minutes from home, he was stopped by a female state trooper. Dave got out of his car and identified himself as a contributor to the Police Benevolent Fund and an auxiliary police officer. He was expecting "officer courtesy" from what he perceived to be a fellow officer.

The trooper asked Dave for his proof of insurance and driver's license. Unwisely, he refused, stating who he was. The trooper informed Dave she didn't care who he was. That's when Dave became irate, and a heated argument ensued. And he still refused to give the trooper his license and proof of insurance.

Eventually, backup troopers arrived and Dave was booked for DUI and placed in the county lockup. He was also charged with resisting arrest.

The moral of this story is not that Dave should have been given officer courtesy, but that Dave's management style of himself and other people had been arbitrary his whole life. He rarely attended to the needs and requests of other people, and yet he expected everyone else to continually attend to *his* needs and requests. When Dave experienced someone like himself, he became angry and combative. If Dave had developed effective management skills, he might have prevented the above situation. He also might have preserved his marriage and family. Dave's poor managing skills of himself and others led to his demise.

Managing behavior simply refers to the actions and responses that both partners use to meet their individual needs and the needs of each other. Without the ability to manage your personal needs, your personal relationships can get out of balance. If our partner always wants his/her way and tends to deny our needs in the process, we may become angry or resentful. On the other hand, there are times when we may not be able to grant the needs of our partner's. That must also be managed skillfully.

There are two sub-skills in Managing our own needs and the needs of our partners: Handling Requests and Making Requests.

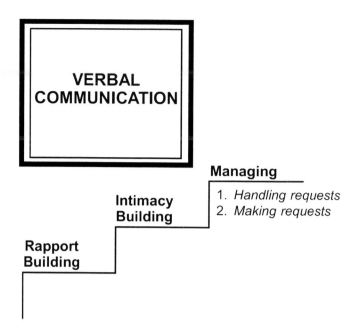

VERBAL COMMUNICATION

Intimacy Building

Managing
1. *Handling requests*
2. *Making requests*

Rapport Building

These skills are more likely to work with our partners if all the skills discussed previously are utilized in our personal relationships. In other words, people are more likely to grant our requests, or needs, if the relationship is on a solid foundation. Conversely, they are more likely to accept our inability to handle their requests, or needs, if the relationship is secure.

Making the Point—The RIGHT Way
The Case of Requesting Right

Mia and Aman have been married for 20 years. They have a very positive relationship. They have had their ups and downs, but they have weathered them with poise and class throughout the years. They are sitting at the kitchen table. Their three children are not home.

Aman: Would you mind if I didn't go with you to your mother's house this weekend? I really want to watch the football game between the Cowboys and the Giants with Rod and Ernesto. We've got a small bet on it. *(making a request)*

Mia: No, I'm fine with that. I know Dad doesn't like football, so be with your friends. I know it's one of the few things you truly enjoy. *(handling a request)*

(continued)

How to Be in a Personal Relationship

> Since you're going to be home on Sunday, would you mind picking up something for dinner for us and the kids so that I won't have to cook when I get back from my parents'? *(making a request)*
>
> **Aman:** Sure, what would you like? I can pick up pizza, or Chinese, or whatever you like.
>
> **Mia:** You pick it. I know the kids will like either one—you can surprise us. *(handling a request)*
>
> **Aman:** Can you help me next Tuesday? I can't pick up my mother and take her to the grocery store because of that meeting downtown I have to attend. *(making a request)*
>
> **Mia:** No, I have to take my mother to the doctor. I'll get Kate (their daughter) to take your mother to the store. *(handling a request)*

Managing: Handling Requests

Handling requests is the ability to manage requests of others in a fair and effective manner. The skillful handling of requests helps build trust and reduce tension. The two steps in Handling Requests are Checking Things Out and Giving a Response with a Reason.

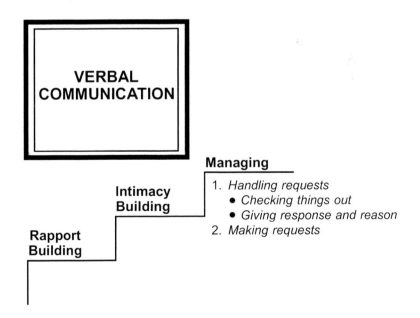

Before we turn to the skills involved in handling requests, we should review the way in which formal and informal rules, rights, and laws often relate to the requests people make and how they may be handled. There are informal and formal rules and laws that govern our behavior. We are also bound by moral values that may or may not have a formal or legal basis. Here are some examples:

Informal Rule: You and your partner have agreed to restrict your spending and follow a budget. The reason you are on this budget is because your partner abused credit cards. The agreement to use a budget is an ***informal*** rule you have both agreed to.

Formal Rule: Your partner asks you to bring home some equipment from your job to be used for personal use. Your company policy clearly states that office equipment is not allowed to leave company premises. This is a ***formal rule or regulation***.

Legal: Your partner thinks it's okay to use illegal drugs because, in your partner's opinion, the use of illegal drugs should be legalized. Your partner wants you to use drugs. Not only do you disagree with your partner's view, but you also refuse to use drugs because it would be breaking the ***law***.

Moral Dilemma: You and your partner are discussing the possibility of your partner going into business with a person whom you don't trust. This other person has made comments in front of you and your partner that support your distrust. For example, this individual has said that it's okay to lie to customers if it gets the job done. Now you have a ***moral dilemma***. Although this person has not broken any formal rules or regulations, you must decide if you want to be in business with a person who has these types of moral ethics.

Of course, many of our requests that we make or handle may not involve any of the above challenges. Most of the time, our ability to meet our needs or the needs of our partner may be the result of everyday circumstances, situations, and events. But it's important to address rules, laws, and morals because if they are part of a request and they are mismanaged, the relationship may be irreparably harmed.

How to Be in a Personal Relationship

Practice

What are two examples of an *informal rule* that would govern a personal relationship you are in?

Example: No smoking in the house; pets live outside.

1. _____

   _____

2. _____

   _____

What are two examples of a *formal rule* you would want established in a personal relationship?

Example: I take care of the inside of the house, and my partner takes care of the outside.

1. _____

   _____

2. _____

   _____

What are two examples of *moral rules* that you want understood in your personal relationship?

Example: It is unacceptable to lie.

1. _____

   _____

2. _____

   _____

There is always a small chance that a person will react negatively when you can't grant his or her request. But by following some simple steps, you can increase the possibility of getting others to respond positively and take away their excuses for negative behavior—even in the eyes of the people who want to see you as acting unfair or arbitrary toward them.

Checking Things Out. While responding to any request, you need to use your nonverbal and mental attending skills to check out the person making the request. Is your partner leveling with you? Or is he or she trying to deceive you? You also need to check out the situation. In other words, what rules might apply? You may also use rapport-building skills. As you practice, this will become much clearer to you.

Making the Point—The RIGHT Way
The Case of Turning Down Tom

Zoë and Tom have been dating for several months. They are planning on marriage in the next year. Zoë came from a family that is financially secure. She works for her father's company and is expected to take over when he retires. Tom, on the other hand, has struggled his whole life to achieve financial security. He is a hard worker, but wants some material things in his life that he's never had. Recently, Tom saw a motorcycle that he wants to purchase. It's been his dream. He approaches Zoë about purchasing it, but she is reluctant to agree.

Tom: I really want to buy that motorcycle. I've worked hard and it's always been my dream.

Zoë: No, I don't think it's a good idea. You and I both agreed that we would save our money and purchase a house right after we get married.

Tom: I know, but this is something I really want. Besides, we'll eventually have the money to buy the house when you take over your dad's company.

Zoë: Tom, you and I agreed that my family having money wasn't going to be an excuse to buy things that we couldn't afford on our own.

Tom: All right, I agree.

Zoë: Look, I know it's important to you, but it's not just the money. I love you, and I don't want you on a motorcycle—they're dangerous!

HANDLING REQUESTS means *checking things out*
by sizing up the person and the situation.

Practice

1. How might you feel if you were Tom?

    Feeling word: _____

2. What message would it communicate if this kind of exchange happened often where Zoë frequently denies Tom's requests, legitimately or not?

    _____

    _____

    _____

    _____

    _____

3. How might it affect Tom's attitude toward Zoë?

    _____

    _____

    _____

    _____

    _____

Occasionally, there will be situations where regulations or rules are not enough to decide if a request can or should be granted. You may need to consider the following questions before granting or not granting a request:

- Does a basic need or right apply to the request that goes beyond the formal rules, the informal rules, or the regulations?

    Example: *Your partner's family needs financial help due to serious and unexpected illness. You and your partner have agreed to stay on a budget so that you can purchase a home next year, but you also share the belief that family members should help one another.*

- Does the partner's special circumstances or past behaviors apply to the request?

    Example: *You and your partner always spend every other holiday season with your family. This year, you are planning the holiday with your family, and your partner, who rarely makes requests, asks if you would consider spending this year with* *your partner's family because his/her parent is not doing well medically.*

- Are there situational circumstances, beyond rules, that might apply to granting or not granting the request?

  Example: *Your partner has just received information that his/her child from a previous relationship is ill and the ex-spouse needs extra money to pay for the child's medical needs that go beyond what was decreed in the divorce.*

HANDLING REQUESTS means *checking things out* and deciding if the request is legitimate or not.

To summarize, when checking things out, use your:

1. Nonverbal attending skills of arranging, positioning, posturing, gesturing, facing, vocalizing, appearing, touching

2. Mental attending skills of observing and listening

3. Emotion management skills of recognizing emotions, reasoning, and relating emotions to others

4. Managing skills for handling and making requests. Determine:
    - What rules apply to the request
    - If a basic need or right applies to the request
    - If there are special circumstances or past behaviors that apply to the request
    - If there are situational factors that apply to the request

Now you're ready to respond to the request itself.

Giving Response and Reason. This skill involves indicating the action you're going to take and giving your partner the reasons for your decision. Responding to your partner with a good reason is a sign of respect.

RESPONDING with a *reason* is respectful.

Basically, you have three possible avenues of action in relation to a request. In each case, you should give some reason for your action. Here are some formats that can be used:

Yes   "Yes, I'll do __(request)__ ."

No   "No, I can't do __(request)__ because __(reason)__ ."

Maybe "I'm not sure if I can __(request)__ because __(reason)__ ."

Making the Point—The RIGHT Way
The Case of Pushy Peter

Karen and Peter have been dating for a couple of months. Peter has been pressuring Karen for sex. Karen doesn't want to have sex for the sake of sex. She is not a virgin, but she believes she has to feel comfortable with someone before she has sex with him. Below is their dialogue one evening after going out on a date:

Peter: I can't believe you think it's such a big deal about having sex. We've been going out for a couple of months. *(making a request)*

Karen: I keep telling you no because it's the rule I've set for myself. I have to feel comfortable, and I have to tell you, your continuing to press me about this is making it even more difficult for me. *(handling a request)*

Peter: (Feeling guilty) I'm sorry. I guess I need to just back off. *(rapport building)*

Karen: I know you're frustrated. It's just something I've always done for me when I've just met someone. *(rapport building)*

DVD

MANAGING: Handling Requests
— The *Wrong* Way and the *Right* Way

Practice

List three legitimate requests your partner might make of you.

Example: He/she wants to borrow your car.

1. _____
   _____

2. _____
   _____

3. _____
   _____

List three requests your partner might make that you would not grant and the reasons why (**Note:** Keep in mind that your particular circumstances and relationship history could determine your answers).

Example:

Request: My partner asked me to lie to our friends about why we haven't been spending time with them.

Why I can't grant the request: I care about my friends, but they are always inconsiderate of our needs, and we need to explain that to them rather than avoid them.

1. Request: _____

   Why denied: _____

   _____

2. Request: _____

   Why denied: _____

   _____

3. Request: _____

   Why denied: _____

   _____

Action Strategies

Below are some Handling Requests Strategies you may want to use in your personal relationships if the situation allows for it.

1. The next time your partner asks you to do something that you are unable to do because of time or other obligations, practice the following steps:

    *   Nonverbally Attend.

    *   Mentally Attend.

    *   Respond and Ask Questions before handling the request (if applicable).

    *   Say, "No I can't __(request)__ because __(reason)__."

    *   Say, "I'm sorry," and respond to their feelings.

2. The next time your partner asks you to do something that goes against some predetermined rule that you both agreed upon earlier in your relationship, practice the following steps:

    *   Nonverbally Attend.

    *   Mentally Attend.

    *   Respond and Ask Questions before handling the request (if applicable).

    *   Say, "No, I can't __(request)__ because __(reason)__, and you and I agreed that we/I would not __(request)__."

    *   Say, "I'm sorry" (respond to their feelings), and then say, "I know you're probably __(mad, hurt, frustrated)__ (what they are feeling) because I can't say, 'Yes!' but I think it's important we stick to our agreement."

Now, write a Handling Requests Action Strategy:

_____

_____

_____

_____

_____

Managing: Making Requests

Making requests is the ability to make specific requests of your partner. Making requests *skillfully* improves the chances that your partner will cooperate and more readily meet your needs. The two skills involved in Making Requests effectively are Checking Things Out, using the same procedures as when you are handling requests, and Taking Appropriate Action.

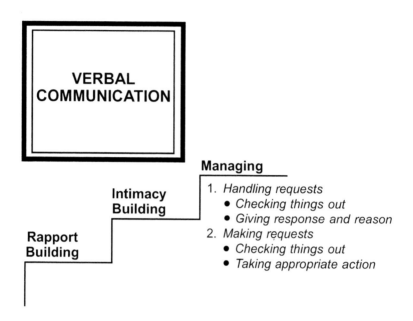

Checking Things Out. As with handling requests, you need to check things out to make sure that you don't make the wrong move—a move that might increase tension rather than calm things down. Once you've done this, you decide what kind of action you need to make when making the request that will increase the chances your request will be granted.

Making the Point—The WRONG Way
The Case of Now or Never

Christina and Rodney have been married for two years. Christina is a very demanding person at times, and when she wants something badly, it's "her way or the highway"! Rodney has become really annoyed with Christina's demands. He has decided that he has had enough and, if she does it again, he's going to confront her about it.

It is Tuesday evening. Rodney, a self-employed cabinetmaker, is in his workshop finishing up a project for a very important customer. Christina has just walked downstairs to make a request of Rodney.

Christina: (Yelling because Rodney is running one of his power tools) Rodney! Rodney! Rodney! (Rodney shuts down his power tool) Look, I want you to come upstairs and take the trash out to the curb. It's Tuesday night. You know trash pickup is tomorrow. I get tired of having to remind you. *(making a request)*

Rodney: Look, I'll do it as soon as I finish this project. I've got to get this finished tonight so that I can get paid tomorrow. *(handling a request)*

Christina: (Angry tone and facial expression) I want it done NOW, not later! (She then storms out of Rodney's workshop) *(making a request)*

Rodney: (Yelling as she leaves the workshop) I'll get it done when I get it done! *(handling a request)*

Christina: (Turns toward him and puts a hand on her hip) What do you mean, "When I get it done"?

Rodney: (Deciding he's had it) Look, I've had it with you talking to me like I'm your servant. You're not helpless. Take out the trash yourself. As a matter of fact, the physical exercise might do you some good. Get off my back, 'cause you know what? If you'd learn to respect the fact that what I'm doing makes us a living that allows you and me to have a life, you would realize that whether I take out the trash now or at 11 o'clock tonight makes absolutely no difference!

Since the skills here will be the same as those involved in Handling Requests, there's no need to go back over them. As a matter of fact, this is a good time to go to the "Checking Things Out" section under "Handling Requests" for a quick review. However, when checking things out before making requests, your aim should be to understand as much as possible about the situation. In other words, ask the question, "How will making this request impact my partner?" Is your partner willing to do the request? Will your partner feel like he/she is losing face if you give him/her some direction and react antagonistically? Is your partner in the midst of doing something already? If so, should you interrupt them?

By using your Nonverbal and Mental Attending skills, you will increase the chances that your partner will respond positively to your request without increasing tension.

> **MAKING REQUESTS** means *checking things out*
> using your nonverbal and mental attending skills,
> along with your emotion management, rapport-
> building, and managing skills to evaluate the
> appropriateness of the request and the impact
> the request will have on others.

Taking Appropriate Action. Making requests of partners is obviously a routine part of personal relationships. Many requests are made throughout the life of a relationship, and too often little thought is given to the impact of the request on the partner and the partner's immediate and long-term cooperation. More often than not, it is *how* the request is made that makes the difference, not the nature of the request.

> **MAKING REQUESTS** means *taking appropriate action*
> by selecting the best way to make your request.

In taking action to get a partner to do something, you have to be specific. You should identify what you want done and when you need it done by. Making a request using this guideline keeps the communication clear. We have found that a polite request of your partner is the best approach. Although you may occasionally find that an assertive or confrontational format is justified or necessary, it is best to avoid them when possible.

MAKING REQUEST FORMATS

Civil Format (Mild)
    "Would you __(request)__ because __(reason)__?"

Assertive Format (Moderate)
    "I want you to __(request)__ because __(reason)__."

Confrontational Format (Strong)
    "I want you to __(request)__ now." (This request is for immediate action and may or may not include a reason.)

You may be in a situation where your mental-attending skills tell you that making the request of a partner at a certain point may cause them tension, yet the request has to be made. This would be a good time to use your rapport-building skills to increase the probability that your request will be met without unnecessary tension.

Making the Point—The RIGHT Way
The Case of the Give-and-Take Couple

Jenna and Chip have been married for eight years. They both have demanding jobs along with two small children. This makes their lives very complicated, especially when you consider the multiple requests they make of each other each day (e.g., Can you pick up the kids? Can you help with the chores?). They have learned that it is in their best interest as a couple to treat each other with civility despite the stress. Here's a typical dialogue between them following dinner with the children.

Jenna: Chip, I know you need to return calls to your customers tonight, but could you help me out by cleaning up the kitchen? I have *got* to help the children with their homework. *(mild request format)*

Chip: (Looking stressed and frustrated) Jenna, I've got to call these people before 9:00 p.m. and it's already 7:00. *(handling request)*

Jenna: (*Nonverbally and mentally attending*) Chip, I know you are tired and stressed, and I'm adding to it, but I need your help. *(rapport building)*

(continued)

Chip:	(Looking like he understands her predicament) Okay, how about this? Why don't you go ahead and help the kids with their homework, and I'll make those business calls before it gets any later. Then we can *both* come back in here and clean up the kitchen. *(mental attending and rapport building)*
Jenna:	(Looking relieved) Sounds like a plan. *(handling request)*
Chip:	(Looking appreciative) Look, I know you feel just as stressed as me. You've got a lot to do, too. *(rapport building)*

Obviously Jenna and Chip have learned how to manage each other's needs with respect and civility. This is not easy when stress levels are high. When stress levels are high, your emotional regulation skills, along with all of the other skills previously addressed in this book, can significantly contribute to the success of your making and handling requests skillfully.

DVD

MANAGING: Making Requests
— The *Wrong* Way and the *Right* Way

Practice

There may be times when you might have to be assertive, or even confrontive, with your partner. List three examples below where you might need to make a moderate (assertive) or strong (confrontive) request of your partner.

Example: Your partner continues to tease you in front of guests or friends, even though you have asked your partner not to.

1. _____

_____

2. _____

_____

3. _____

_____

Action Strategies

Below are some Making Requests Strategies you may want to use in your personal relationships if the situation allows for it.

1. The next time you want to ask your partner to do something for you, use the following steps:

    *   Nonverbally attend to your partner.

    *   Mentally attend to your partner to make sure your request should be made.

    *   Make the request using a mild or civil format:

        "Would you mind __(request)__?"

    *   If your partner seems reluctant to grant your request, restate the request while giving a reason.

        "Would you mind __(request)__ because __(reason)__?"

    *   If your partner still seems hesitant, use your rapport-building skills.

        Respond to feeling: "You look reluctant."
        Ask a relevant question: "Is this a bad time to ask?"

2. Your partner continues to ignore a request you have made of them, despite numerous attempts on your part to use a civil approach. You decide you need to use a stronger request format (assertive).

    *   Nonverbally attend to your partner.

    *   Mentally attend to your partner to make sure your request should be made.

    *   Make the request using a mild or civil format:

        "Would you please __(request)__ because __(reason, and include the fact that you have made the request before)__?"

    *   If your partner continues to act indifferent, make the request using a "moderate" format (assertive):

        "I want you to __(request)__ because __(reason)__?"

Answers to the Emotional Vocabulary Practice on p. 154

Category of Emotion	High Intensity	Moderate Intensity	Low Intensity
Happy	intoxicated captivated ecstatic exultant joyous jubilant thrilled overjoyed	lively gay cheerful gleeful delighted elated joyful peppy tickled upbeat	merry light jolly glad blissful chipper content perky playful up
Sad	grieved gloomy heartbroken bereaved despairing despondent heavy-hearted	downcast forlorn cheerless glum heartsick hurting melancholy	down blue low somber sorry
Scared	overwhelmed alarmed fearful petrified terrified panicked	worried shaky tense afraid anxious panicky shaken	startled surprised uneasy edgy apprehensive hesitant
Angry	ferocious irate hostile hateful incensed maddened outraged raging storming fuming	annoyed sullen sulky provoked offended fuming ticked off mad aggravated irritated irked	perturbed hassled bothered

(continued)

How to Be in a Personal Relationship

Answers to the Emotional Vocabulary Practice on p. 154
(concluded)

Category of Emotion	High Intensity	Moderate Intensity	Low Intensity
Confused	bewildered disoriented stunned baffled perplexed muddled disconnected	befuddled doubtful distracted disorganized puzzled helpless	baffled dazed misled undecided uncertain lost
Strong	active hearty mighty unyielding vigorous powerful potent fearless forceful ferocious	hardy hefty robust tough brave sound daring	capable adequate firm able assured solid stable steady content
Weak	ashamed anemic decrepit frail exhausted powerless depleted	fragile sluggish spent wavering wobbly worn out vulnerable inept inadequate run down	feeble limp soft wimpy unable tired weary

Skills Summary
Verbal Communication

Now let's review all of the skills and sub-skills involved in Verbal Communication.

VERBAL COMMUNICATION

Managing

1. *Handling requests*
   - *Checking things out*
   - *Giving response and reason*
2. *Making requests*
   - *Checking things out*
   - *Taking appropriate action*

Intimacy Building

1. *Self-disclosure*
   - *Knowing the guidelines*
   - *Knowing the types of disclosures*
   - *Expressing disclosures*
   - *Receiving disclosures*
2. *Reinforcing*
   - *Verbally*
   - *Nonverbally*

   Nonreinforcing
   - *Verbally*
   - *Nonverbally*

Rapport Building

1. *Responding techniques*
   - *Content*
     - *Reflect on what was seen and heard*
     - *Use a responding format to respond to content*
   - *Feeling*
     - *Reflect on feeling*
     - *Reflect on feeling and intensity*
   - *Meaning*
     - *Reflect on feeling and reason for that feeling*
     - *Respond to the feeling and meaning*
2. *Asking relevant questions*
   - *Using the 5WH method*
   - *Reflecting on answers and recycling*

How to Be in a Personal Relationship

Prologue

Congratulations! You've just completed learning the skills necessary to have a healthy, maintained personal relationship. We hope that you have found this material helpful and easy to understand as well as easy to implement with your partner. Remember, as with any skill, practice makes perfect. The more you practice these skills, the more "natural" they will become. And, like any skill, you choose what skill to use when, where, how, why, and with whom. Having these skills adds to the number of options you have when handling any situation. As we said in the Introduction, without these skills, your options are more limited.

So keep this book handy, refer back to it as you become more skilled in your communications and interactions with your partner, and enjoy your new fundamental skills for loving!